The Little-Known Pika

Also by ROBERT T. ORR

The Animal Kingdom

Animals in Migration

The American pika (*Ochotona princeps*).
(*Photograph by Douglas B. Herr*)

The Little-Known Pika

by ROBERT T. ORR

MACMILLAN PUBLISHING CO., INC.

NEW YORK

COLLIER MACMILLAN PUBLISHERS

LONDON

Macmillan Publishing Co., Inc.
866 Third Avenue, New York, N.Y. 10022
Collier Macmillan Canada, Ltd.

Library of Congress Cataloging in Publication Data

Orr, Robert Thomas, 1908-
    The little-known pika.

    Bibliography: p.
    Includes index.
    1. Pikas.   I. Title.
QL737.L33077   599'.322   77-9301
ISBN 0-02-593960-2

FIRST PRINTING 1977

Unless otherwise noted, all photographs are by
Robert T. Orr.

Printed in the United States of America

Dedicated to my wife

MARGARET

who spent many long, uncomfortable hours
patiently waiting with me on mountain rockslides
so that we might learn more about the habits
of pikas.

Contents

Introduction

THE SECTION OF THE forest where the trail started was dominated by large Jeffrey pines, many of which had reached their maximum growth. Intermingled and more numerous were white firs, so typical of this part of the Sierra Nevada. As the morning warmed up, the sweet vanilla scent characteristic of the pine bark filled the air. It was August and long past the blooming season in the lowlands, but here, at 6,500 feet, wildflowers were still at their peak. Higher up the mountain slope the season would just be starting. In open spaces, between clumps of tobacco brush and manzanita, the brilliant red flowers of the skyrocket gilia dazzled the eye. Nearby were the large, yellow, sunflowerlike blooms of wyethia, often called mule ears because of the large, hairy, gray leaves shaped somewhat like the ears of a mule.

The songs of the territorial birds were much less noticeable than they had been a month ago. The monotonous call of the wood pewee

was still repeated endlessly, but only on rare occasions could one hear
the loud notes of the olive-sided flycatcher that periodically sallied
forth from its treetop perch. The daybreak chorus of robins had de-
creased greatly in the past several weeks and many young, their
breasts still spotted, could be seen foraging like adults.

As we continued climbing toward the high country, whose snow-
capped peaks could occasionally be glimpsed through the trees,
there was a gradual change in the plant life. Lodgepole pines, still
called tamaracks by some old timers, became more abundant, especially where it was damp and shady. White firs, so common lower
down, were not found as often. In their place was another species,
the red fir. This is a stately tree that grows to a height of as much
as 175 feet. Its bark is dark red in old trees, and the foliage is often
so dense that sunlight can scarcely penetrate. Occasionally intermingled with these firs were western white pines, their pendant
cones resembling those of sugar pines, but nowhere as large.

Once in the red fir-white pine forest, one has the feel of the high
mountains. The air is rarer. The sky seems a deeper blue. There is
more silence, occasionally broken by the high-pitched song of the
golden-crowned kinglet, a species closely related to the goldcrest
of the boreal forests of Eurasia. We hoped we might see or hear the
cry of a goshawk, that magnificent predator of the high fir belt, but
no such luck. We did, however, startle a blue grouse on which the
goshawk preys. The sudden rapid whir of wings as this large
gallinaceous bird flew off was an exciting sound.

Higher still the forest became more open, with large patches of
white phlox. Some of these diminutive plants that so closely hug
the earth were quite old, and their resemblance to bonsais has made
them collectors' items. Brilliant blue pentstemon and scarlet paint-
brush made a vivid contrast with this ground cover. Mountain hemlocks were now appearing, each with the leader at the tip of its
trunk bent over in characteristic fashion.

Besides these changes in the plant life, the land itself showed differences. The trail wound around huge granite boulders, and small ponds from recently melted snow were scattered about. There was a sheer cliff ahead with a great mass of broken granite at its base. This talus sloped downward at an angle of about thirty degrees and terminated in a small glacial lake. Some of the rocks were twenty feet across and weighed many tons. Others were small or of medium size. The adjacent slopes were clothed with subalpine herbs and shrubs, many with succulent leaves and stems, others laden with berries. This is what we had come for and where we would make our camp for the night.

Suddenly two sharp, barklike notes came from somewhere among the rocks. By remaining motionless, carefully scanning the slope for a few minutes, we saw a small, grayish brown animal with a stocky body, no visible tail, and small rounded ears. It was sitting alert on a large granite slab that slanted backward and was partly protected by an overhanging boulder. More barks were heard farther up the slope. By patient waiting, we began to see others, also on the alert. Occasionally one would move toward the edge of the talus and out to the adjacent vegetation to feed. Sometimes one would return with a great clump of plant material in its mouth. We watched as it was placed on a pile of vegetation that had already been collected and looked like a small haystack among the rocks. It was not a community effort, and any intrusion toward a haypile by a neighbor resulted in a chase.

What were these strange little creatures that lived in such a rugged and remote environment and had such interesting habits? Those who know them call them pikas. They are members of the same group of mammals as hares and rabbits, the Lagomorpha. This story is about their world, how it changes, and how the pika's behavior changes during the four seasons of the year.

The Little-Known Pika

History and Relationship of Pikas

T HE NAME PIKA is derived from the word *puka*, the name given a group of small subarctic mammals by the Tungus, a tribe that lives in northeastern Siberia. Various other vernacular names have been applied to these animals, such as rock rabbits, little chief hares, and conies. Their similarity to a diminutive hare or rabbit accounts for the first two names, and one familiar with the Old World conies might see a resemblance between these two groups of animals. True conies, however, are members of a small order of Asiatic and African mammals called the Hyracoidea. These are probably more closely related to elephants than to pikas, to which they bear only a superficial resemblance.

The first known pikas were described in 1769 by Peter Simon Pallas, a Prussian naturalist, from specimens taken in southern Siberia and eastern Russia. Because of their obvious relationship to members of the order Lagomorpha, they were placed in the same

1

genus as the hare and named *Lepus pusillus*. In 1795, D. H. F.
Link placed them in a new genus, *Ochotona*. Unfortunately this
name was overlooked for more than a century and unearthed only in
1896 by the renowned British mammalogist Oldfield Thomas. In
North America the first pika was described in 1828 by John Richardson from specimens collected near the headwaters of the Athabaska
River in western Canada. Richardson called it *Lepus princeps*,
following Pallas' belief that it was a small hare. Many other populations of North American pikas were subsequently described, some
being considered separate species; but currently only the collared
pika (*Ochotona collaris*) of Alaska and northwestern Canada, described in 1893 by Edward W. Nelson, is regarded as a species
distinct from *Ochotona princeps*. Because of the broken distribution
of pikas in western North America, many genetically isolated populations of *Ochotona princeps* are given subspecific recognition.

Why the pika is in a different family from the hare and rabbit
can be seen in their physical characteristics. The most obvious
features of hares and rabbits are their large ears and proportionately
long hind legs. Pikas have small rounded ears and their hind legs
are only slightly larger than the front ones. Even the smallest species
of rabbit is considerably larger than a pika, whose body length does
not exceed eight inches. Hares and rabbits have short but distinct
tails while pikas lack a visible tail. Another marked difference between the two groups relates to vocalization. Hares and rabbits are
notably silent except when captured or injured, when they will
scream. Pikas are quite vocal and utter a single or series of short
barks or bleats as a means of communication.

The family Ochotonidae appears to have had its origin in Asia,
where today twelve of the fourteen living species occur. No pikas
are known south of the Himalayas, but they range in the Old World
from eastern Siberia and Korea, south through Mongolia to southwestern China and Tibet, then west to Uzbekistan, Afghanistan,

Iran, and the Ural Mountains of southeastern Europe. One kind is found in Japan, on the island of Hokkaido.

Of the two species of pikas found in North America, one is restricted to parts of southeastern Alaska, the Yukon Territory, and extreme northern British Columbia. This is the northern or collared pika (*Ochotona collaris*) seen by visitors to Mt. McKinley. Its common name originates from the distinct grayish patch on the shoulders and nape of the neck. The fur on the underparts of the body is white. Farther south, in western Canada and the United States, the southern pika (*Ochotona princeps*) is found in parts of the Rocky Mountains, Pacific Coast ranges, Cascades, and Sierra Nevada, as well as on certain isolated mountain ranges in the Great Basin. It lacks the grayish collar and the fur on the belly has a buff tint. The two species, however, are so close that some scientists believe the northern form should be regarded as a subspecies of the more widespread and earlier-named *Ochotona princeps*; thus giving it the technical name of *Ochotona princeps collaris*. The vernacular term "North American pika" could then be used collectively for all New World populations.

The fur of all pikas is soft and silky, very much like that of rabbits, and, like them, the feet and toes are well furred. This is a distinct advantage to an animal living in a cold environment. The skin is almost paper-thin, but the soft, thick fur compensates for this.

Pikas have two molts a year during which the old fur is lost and replaced by new. In the American species of pikas, the first molt begins in late June or early July and is completed within a couple of weeks. It begins on the head and progresses over the body, often in an irregular manner. The winter pelage, usually acquired during the month of September in a manner similar to that of the summer, is heavier than the summer coat.

The molt of the various Eurasian species seems to follow the same pattern as *Ochotona princeps*. It has been noted by Russian authors that the fur on the nape of the neck is the last to be replaced and that males molt earlier than females. This delay in females appears to be correlated with reproductive activity.

Fossil records of pikas go as far back as the Oligocene in Europe and Asia, and remains of these animals are known from the Miocene in Africa and North America. The family Ochotonidae therefore originated more than thirty million years ago, and was well into many parts of the world twenty-five million years ago. No one knows in what sort of habitat these ancient pikas lived, but they have long been separated from their nearest relatives, the hares and rabbits of the family Leporidae.

The two families, Ochotonidae and Leporidae, constitute a distinct mammalian order, the Lagomorpha. Hares and rabbits are far better known than the diminutive pikas. Even the name of the order comes from the Greek meaning "hare-shaped." Although the group has long been confused with rodents, members of the two orders have very little in common. The trademark of a rodent is the incisors, front teeth, of which they have two above and two below. Lagomorphs have four incisors above, two of which are small and behind the larger front two, and two in the lower jaw. The rodent incisors have enamel restricted to the front surface, whereas the crowns of lagomorph incisors are completely surrounded by enamel. The lower jaw of a rodent moves forward and backward in the process of chewing because of the shape of the articulation with the skull; a lagomorph's jaw motion is lateral. There are also marked differences in the reproductive systems of the two orders. Male rodents possess a baculum, penis bone, which is absent in lagomorphs. Ovulation in female lagomorphs, unlike female rodents, is induced by copulation. Other morphological and physiological differences support paleontological evidence indicating that lagomorphs and rodents have been distinct for a vast period of time.

This sloping mass of talus in the central
Sierra Nevada is home for a small pika colony.

It seems logical to assume that Recent pikas reached North America by way of a land bridge between Asia and Alaska across the Bering Strait. *Ochotona princeps* and *collaris* are closely related and probably became distinct from one another in the late Pleistocene as a result of geographic separation. They are members of the subgenus *Pika* to which many of the pikas of Asia and southeastern Europe belong. These were not the first members of their family to inhabit the North American continent. Remains have been found of pikas who lived here over fifteen million years ago. Perhaps there were others even earlier whose fossilized remains are yet to be discovered by paleontologists. They, too, may have come from Asia, but it is possible that they came through land connections with Europe. The story of their origin is still unsolved. We know nothing of their habits or habitat. One suspects they may have lived in burrows in forests or on steppes, like some of the living Asiatic species.

To be restricted to rockslides, like modern North American pikas, would not seem to favor movement across continents or from one continent to another. One can speculate, though, that during the Pleistocene our North American pikas were rather widely distributed over the cooler lowlands of this continent, where they may have lived in burrows in the open. With the ultimate recession of the glaciers and the accumulation of water in the lowlands, they were forced higher and higher into the mountains and found protection in talus produced by glacial action. Food was found adjacent to these areas. The result was genetic isolation of populations on different peaks and mountain ranges, thereby creating what are essentially many island subspecies.

The Environment

NORTH AMERICA

Most pikas in North America live in mountain-ous terrain, although there are exceptions, as in western British Columbia where some colonies have been found near sea level. Rocks are an essential part of their environment. These may be talus slopes (broken rocks at the base of a cliff), isolated rockslides resulting from the weathering of larger masses, or even scattered lava piles. Some pikas have taken over slab piles left by lumber operations and others have been found inhabiting burrows a short distance from rock.

The use of burrows in or immediately adjacent to rockslides is not uncommon, although the removal of rocks from some inhabited sites has shown that the animals may have nests of vegetation deep under the talus but not necessarily in holes in the ground.

Since rocks provide both home and protection for most pikas, they must be of the proper size. If the rocks are too small, the crevices are

7

A diversity of rock sizes provide good
lookouts and prevent large predators from
penetrating the crevices.

inadequate for passage. If they are too big, larger predators will have easy access to this small animal. The optimum size, therefore, must be such that the pika may move freely through the complicated maze of passageways in the rock pile but will prevent larger animals from penetrating too far. This does not necessarily mean a uniformity of rock size, but rather a maximum and minimum in size of the passageways. Variation in rock size seems desirable, since a certain number of large rocks are needed to provide favorable sites for lookouts and the large overhanging slabs offer cover for the drying of winter haypiles.

In very extensive rockslides, only the peripheral areas are inhabited since these are closest to the adjacent feeding areas. As one progresses inward from the edge of a broad talus, the population density of the pikas decreases. Because of this, there are higher population densities on small insular rockslides than on large rocky areas.

The presence or absence of pikas is sometimes a surprise. I have found very favorable-looking sites in pika country that showed no sign of their presence. On the other hand, they sometimes occur where least expected. According to the late Arthur H. Howell, mammalogist with the former U.S. Bureau of Biological Survey, it was not until 1921 that isolated colonies of pikas were discovered living in scattered lava piles in the sagebrush desert country of southern Idaho in what is now Craters of the Moon National Monument.

Proper temperature and an adequate food supply adjacent to rock piles appear to be of prime importance for the presence of this species in a particular area. There are only a few instances of pikas being found away from middle and higher mountain elevations. These are in the northwest Pacific Coast where the climate is cool and colonies occasionally occur in rockslides near sea level, and in the northern Great Basin region where they have been found in piles of lava rock. In the latter area, which is a high cool desert, the summers are short and the temperature remains very low for many months of the year. Such isolated colonies as do occur here are few and may represent relict populations that were much more extensive in the late Pleistocene.

Pika colonies may be found in areas over 13,500 feet in parts of the Rocky Mountains and the Sierra Nevada. They are most common at or above timberline and are rarely encountered below 6,000 feet. Alpine meadows adjacent to rocky slopes offer an abundant food supply during the summer and fall months at the higher elevations.

Food is essential to a suitable environment. One encounters many rockslides in our western mountains that would provide adequate cover, but the absence of necessary food plants adjacent to them inhibits occupancy. Fortunately, the pikas in North America enjoy a broad range of food plants.

Although all pika rockslides must have certain basic elements in common, no two are exactly alike. One colony, at an elevation of 6,600 feet in the central Sierra Nevada, that I have kept under observation for more than forty years is in a talus that slopes downhill for about 150 feet from the base of a 500-foot granite cliff. Its width averages about thirty feet, and it is composed of broken rocks ranging from one to ten feet in greatest dimensions. On either side of the slide is low, but dense, vegetation dominated by bitter cherry (*Prunus emarginata*), huckleberry oak (*Quercus vacciniifolia*), two species of manzanita (*Arctostaphylos patula* and *A. nevadensis*), and snowbush (*Ceanothus cordulatus*), along with many smaller shrubs and herbs as well as bracken fern. Scattered Jeffrey pines (*Pinus jeffreyi*) and white firs (*Abies concolor*) are nearby. There are other slides, also inhabited by pikas, on this slope and it is probable that there is movement of individuals from one rockslide to another under the cover of the separating bushy vegetation. This

The pika carefully scrutinizes its
surroundings before moving on.
(*Photograph by Douglas B. Herr*)

would occur especially in late summer when the young of the year are searching for territories.

Another one of my favorite colonies is several miles from this one but at an elevation of 8,000 feet. Here, rising from the shores of a small alpine lake, are two granite rockslides that provide suitable cover for pikas. At this higher altitude, however, the vegetation is different, being composed of mountain ash (*Sorbus sitchensis*), Labrador tea (*Ledum glandulosum*), serviceberry (*Amelanchier alnifolia*), squaw currant (*Ribes cereum*), with some red heather (*Phyllodoce breweri*). Scattered about are conifers including mountain hemlock (*Tsuga mertensiana*), western white pine (*Pinus monticola*), lodgepole pine (*Pinus contorta* var. *murrayana*), red fir (*Abies magnifica*), and an occasional western juniper (*Juniperus occidentalis*).

Higher still in the Sierra Nevada, near the headwaters of the North Fork of the San Joaquin River, I spent a week above timberline at 11,500 feet where pikas abounded in many, very extensive, rockslides. Where these slides met moist meadows, alpine willow (*Salix petrophila*), red heather (*Phyllodoce breweri*), pale laurel (*Kalmia poliifolia*), and white heather (*Cassiope mertensiana*) were the dominant low-growing shrubs, with numerous small herbaceous plants scattered among the rocks.

These three pika habitats indicate the wide diversity of plant life at different elevations that may be associated with a suitable rockslide area in the central Sierra Nevada. Similarly, in the Rocky Mountains, pikas range from above timberline, where in many places they are abundant, to small rockslides scattered about the coniferous forests lower down.

A typical Rocky Mountain pika colony visited several years ago near Missoula, Montana, was in an open area surrounded by a Douglas fir (*Pseudotsuga menziesii*)-ponderosa pine (*Pinus ponderosa*) forest. On either side and at the lower edge of the basaltic

Broken rock, intermingled with vegetation
suitable for pikas, becomes more abundant
above 8,000 feet in the Sierra Nevada.

rockslide, the dominant non-coniferous plants were mountain cranberry (*Vaccinium vitis-idaea*), Oregon grape (*Berberis repens*),
wild raspberry (*Rubus strigosus*), Utah twin flower (*Lonicera
utahensis*), lungwort (*Mertensia paniculata*), and chokecherry
(*Prunus virginiana* var. *demissa*). This was but one of a number of
rockslides in this region that provided suitable homes for pikas and
had similar plants adjacent.

The pikas of North America, despite their restriction to rockslides,
have adapted themselves to a wide variety of plant species for their
food supply. This accounts for their relatively widespread distribution in the higher mountainous parts of the Pacific Coast and Rocky
Mountain regions where suitable rocky habitats are available.

ASIA

There is a much greater diversity of habitats for the various
species of pikas on the Asiatic continent. Some inhabit rockslides like
their North American counterparts, others live in forests, and some
in open plains away from rocks and trees. Most of these interesting
Old World species live in Siberia, the high mountains of Manchuria
and western China, Tibet, Mongolia, and the central Asiatic Re-
publics of the U.S.S.R.—all regions that, for political reasons, have
been rather inaccessible to American scientists for several decades.

In the 1920s the newspapers and various magazines carried fasci-
nating accounts of the Central Asiatic Expeditions of the American
Museum of Natural History in New York. We read of the exploits
and discoveries made by such famous scientists as Roy Chapman
Andrews, the leader; Walter K. Granger, chief paleontologist and
second in command; Ralph W. Chaney, paleobotanist and later dis-
coverer of the Dawn Redwood; Charles P. Berkey, geologist; Wil-

Pikas, yellow-bellied marmots, and rosy
finches were all abundant in this alpine
environment at 10,500 feet in the south
central Sierra Nevada.

sonal knowledge of pikas in Manchuria, Siberia, and Mongolia has been invaluable, as is his knowledge of the native names applied to them.

We had also read former Chief Justice William O. Douglas' account of his visit to Outer Mongolia in 1961, the year that country became a member of the United Nations. He and his wife, along with a National Geographic staff photographer, were among the first Westerners to visit that remote area in many years.

Loaded with as much information as seemed practical, we left with our group for Central Asia in the latter part of August. Our best chances of finding these animals appeared to be in the Gobi Desert of Outer Mongolia. To get there our trip took us to Khabarovsk via Tokyo and Niigata. Khabarovsk is about 400 miles north of Vladivostok in the Soviet Far East. Here we boarded the Transiberian Railroad and traveled for three days through the steppe and taiga country to Irkutsk in Siberia. Autumn was about to begin and everywhere the birch leaves were turning golden. Irkutsk is on the Angara River, a large tributary of the Yenesei which flows northward through the tundra to the Arctic Ocean. It is the only outlet from Lake Baikal, that great mile-deep body of water that contains one-fifth of the fresh water of the world.

From Irkutsk, with a Russian-speaking American courier from Moscow, we flew south on Aeroflot to Ulan Batar, the capital of the Mongolian People's Republic. We were greeted at the airport by our guide from Zuulchin, the government travel agency. She was a charming and colorfully-garbed intelligent young Mongolian woman named Khu Khu. As soon as we were all assembled, Khu Khu announced that we would leave immediately for the southern Gobi Desert because the climate was at that time favorable. If we were to spend a day or two in Ulan Batar the weather might change and make flying impossible. There were no airfields on the desert so the planes had to land on flat, rock-free areas. I recalled that Roy Chap-

Our yurt quarters in the southwestern Gobi
Desert of Outer Mongolia.

man Andrews had set September 1 as the latest date to leave the
Gobi, as winter blizzards could come any time after this and today
was the first of September. This change in plans was agreeable to
all so off we went on Air Mongol in a Soviet-made Antonov 24. Our
flight took us about 400 miles southwest of the capital where we
landed one-half mile from a village. There we were met by two
small buses which took us another twenty-two miles south to our
yurt camp.

The yurt, used by Mongols for centuries, is a round, felted tent
about twenty-five feet in diameter with a cone-shaped roof supported
by narrow strips of wood. The strips are painted bright colors, and
the inside walls are hung with colorful cloth. The floor is covered
with rugs, and the beds are arranged around the sides. In the center
of each yurt is a small wood stove with a chimney rising through a
hole in the center of the wigwamlike top. There are no windows,
only a door and the hole in the roof. We found these accommodations
to be exceedingly comfortable, much more so than Siberian hotels.
The construction and shape of the yurt is such that it needs no outside support and offers no flat surface to resist the strong winds of
the Gobi. It also helps to exclude the cold of winter when a temperature of −50° F. is not uncommon.

From our camp we could look to the southwest and see a range of
mountains about 9,000 feet high. This was the Artsa Bogdo, the
southern end of the Altai Mountains, an enormous range that extends
in a great arc from the southwestern edge of the Gobi Desert northwest and then north to Siberia. It serves as a barrier separating
Mongolia from China's Sinkiang Province and the Tibetan Plateau
to the south, and from the Central Asiatic Republic of Kazakhstan
to the west. Everywhere, except toward the mountains, the land was
flat with a covering of low sparse vegetation dominated in places by
a species of small wild onion. We knew that the famous dinosaur
digs and Flaming Cliffs were no more than fifty miles away.

The only lagomorph to visit our camp was *Lepus tolai*, the Asiatic counterpart of the jack rabbit, *Lepus californicus*, of western North America.

There were no signs of pikas in the flat, sparsely-grown desert near our camp, but we did have one of their relatives greet us. This was a large hare (*Lepus tolai*) which lived under one of the yurts and allowed fairly close approach. We later saw others on the desert and that evening a hedgehog tried to join us in the eating area.

I was not sure what kind of pikas, if any, we might encounter in this region. Dr. Chapman had recorded *Ochotona pallasi* as a common species in the Gobi Desert, but he regarded it as a true rock-loving species, living both in rockslides and in burrows in rocky areas. He also described Daurian pika (*Ochotona daurica*) as a very widespread species in the Gobi Desert where it inhabits grassland, showing preference for long, stiff grass. There the pikas have their burrows and well-marked runways. The Expedition recorded them as occurring widely up to 8,000 feet elevation, but absent from the sandy desert.

Anatole Loukashkin had studied this and another species in Northern Manchuria many years ago and found the Daurian pika living in the high steppes and semi-deserts of the Barga uplands. Their colonies and burrow systems were numerous in grasslands where various herbs were growing, especially *Artemisia*.

Since there were no signs of pikas on the flat desert near our camp or in the dune country fifty miles to the north, where we went one afternoon, our best chance of finding them seemed to be in the Artsa Bogdo. As we ascended this southern end of the Altai Range by car, we climbed from approximately 4,500 feet, on the desert floor, to about 6,500 feet. The plant life gradually changed from the short, sparse grassland dominated by wild onion to one that was much more luxurious, with numerous annual and perennial herbs. Soon the slopes were clothed with a low-growing juniper called *Juniperus sabina*, which closely resembles *Juniperus communis* of the mountains of western North America. The Mongols call it artsa and is responsible for the name of the mountains, the Artsa Bogdo. It is

A high valley in the Artsa Bogdo. Daurian pikas (*Ochotona daurica*) were abundant on the flats and lower slopes where rocks were absent.

said that argali sheep (*Ovis ammon*), which are common here, like to bed down in artsa thickets.

Growing in abundance on the flat canyon bottoms in rich alluvium were such plants as wild celery, rhubarb, mint of several species, senecio, purple aster, iris, yellow yarrow, vetch, a type of loco weed with very inflated pods, sedum, and a beautiful yellow arctic poppy. There was also an abundance of *Artemisia*.

As we drove along, I asked our Mongolian guide if *ogotono* or *ogoton* occurred in these mountains. My pronunciation was not too good but he finally understood my attempt to use the Mongolian words for pika and nodded in the affirmative. A few minutes later my wife spotted what looked like a square blackish rock up a side valley. We decided it was a yak and came to a stop. As we approached the animal on foot I became aware of pika haypiles, burrows, runways, and droppings everywhere on the flat and gentle lower slopes of the narrow valley. I would have forgotten about the yak, even though it was the first I had ever encountered in the wild, if it had not been for the curiosity of one of the ladies of our group who wanted to see how close she could get to it. Since the animal was a bull, and I have great respect for bovine bulls, we did our best to discourage her adventure and get our human flock back into the vehicles. I hastily took some pictures of the yak, the pika colonies, and the general environment before we continued on.

Around the next bend we encountered a herd of yaks and a mile beyond this we stopped for a few hours. While we explored, our drivers and guides prepared a meal by heating rocks in a fire and then placing them in milk cans to cook pieces of meat. The juice provided the soup course which was served after the usual sausage, pickle, and brown bread in Soviet style. A cold Georgian white wine was served with the meat.

Pikas were very abundant in this valley bottom. It was difficult to walk in places without collapsing some of their burrow systems and

A yak bull. In the mountains of central Asia
herds of these animals often graze over areas
inhabited by pikas and compete with them
for food in winter.

The Daurian pika makes very definite runways
through the vegetation leading from
its burrow openings to nearby feeding sites.

haypiles. It was easy to see why the Cossacks in Transbaikalia villages called the animals *senopska* ("haystacker"). The vegetation here was dominated by two species of *Artemisia*. They were short and herblike rather than woody shrubs, as is the Big Basin sagebrush (*Artemisia tridentata*) of western North America. In appearance they more closely resembled diminutive examples of our old man sage (*Artemisia douglasiana*). The genus is a large and complicated one with many species occurring in northern and central Asia. It was of interest to me to note the similarity of the habitat occupied by the Daurian pika in the Altai Mountains of Outer Mongolia to that of the same species in Northern Manchuria, where Loukashkin had also found *Artemisia* to be important.

Unlike *Ochotona princeps* of the rockslides of North America, *Ochotona daurica* is difficult to observe because it moves through runways in the vegetation somewhat like a vole or meadow mouse and is very alert to human presence. Only by my waiting motionless for some minutes would the animals emerge from their burrows. A few individuals had pathways leading down to a small stream that ran through the valley. There they seemed to feed on streamside growth, but the *Artemisia* provided the chief vegetation, being stored in haypiles for winter use. It was an exciting sight to watch these small lagomorphs, along with such birds as white and yellow wagtails and the beautiful isabelline wheatear. From my wife's point of view as a botanist, the most exciting find was an abundance of edelweiss (genus *Leontopodium*) amid the pika colonies. This small composite plant with white, woolly floral leaves and tiny yellow flowers surrounded by silvery bracts is highly prized in Switzerland where it is a symbol of purity and, because of its inaccessibility, is said to have brought death to many who have sought it. It was a beautiful sight growing next to the bright lemon yellow arctic poppies.

A search in the rocky hillsides adjacent to this high valley, known

The entrance to the burrow of a Daurian
pika in open grassland. Note the definite trail.

to the Mongols as the Valley of the Eagles, failed to show the presence of any pikas. I had thought that possibly we might find *Ochotona pallasi* there, but such was not the case. The steep slopes and peaks were the home of the Siberian ibex and the tarbagan or marmot.

Later we went far northward from our yurt camp to the Flaming Cliffs of paleontological fame. We passed many herds of Bactrian camels and saw flocks of Pallas' sandgrouse, that strange bird that periodically has enormous population explosions in central Asia, resulting in some individuals wandering as far northwest as the British Isles. Equally exciting were the occasional greater bustards, game birds almost as large as a turkey, that wander over the desert.

The famous dig was as exciting as expected. On looking over the edge into the red sandstone base, the windcarved rocks reminded me of a miniature of Arizona's Monument Valley. No signs of pikas were to be found, but we did find ancient man-made scraping tools of chipped stone thousands of years old. Our thoughts went back to the days when Genghis Khan, the thirteenth-century Mongol leader, ruled an empire that stretched from China to the Mediterranean. We thought also of the time, over 90 million years ago, when giant reptiles lived here in great swamps. Many changes have taken place with the passage of time.

My one regret when we went westward to the Republic of Kazakhstan was that we had not had the chance to visit the highlands of western China where *Ochotona thibetana* lives. There, at elevations ranging from 10,000 to 16,000 feet, this pika inhabits densely wooded mountains where the dominant vegetation consists of rhododendrons and conifers. It is said to live in burrows and have trails in the dense undergrowth. This is also that part of the world where most of the beautiful species of pheasants occur. A somewhat similar habitat in Manchuria is described by Loukashkin as occupied by the northern pika (*Ochotona hyperborea manchurica*). In the Great

Khinghan Range, this species lives in forests of larch (*Larix dahurica*) where the undergrowth consists mainly of *Rhododendron dahuricum* and thickets of *Vaccinium vitis-idaea*. It inhabits burrows in the dense growth and makes tunnels and paths through the thick layer of moss on the forest floor. Individuals make use of stumps and fallen logs for observation posts.

In other parts of the range, the habitat of the northern pika is quite different. Professor S. I. Ognev, the foremost authority on mammals of the U.S.S.R., states that in Transbaikalia, the area extending from Lake Baikal east to the Amur River and south to Mongolia, this species lives exclusively in screes, masses of detritus and stone or rockslides caused by avalanches or torrents of spring water during times of heavy runoff. Old screes covered with reindeer moss, shrubs, ferns, and other plants are preferred to screes of bare stones. These pikas also inhabit piles of driftwood along creek and river banks. Screes are also their favored habitat in the tundra of northern Siberia.

The alpine pika (*Ochotona alpina*) is also an inhabitant of screes in central Siberia. Three different kinds of screes are described by Ognev. The first is composed of stones caused by disintegration. These accumulate in hollows between larger rocks and are generally on steep, inaccessible slopes. The second type is on rounded mountaintops where broken rocks, resulting from thousands of years of exposure to the elements, are interspersed with plants of the alpine tundra. The third is a simulated scree made by man. In many valleys of the Altai there are ancient tombs of unhewn stone, usually made in the form of a ring. In the center of most of these is a hollow opening into the ground, believed to have been made long ago by grave robbers. Pikas have invaded these tombs which provide them with cover and, as far as they are concerned, resemble a natural scree.

One of the interesting adaptations of this northern pika is that it

Several trails converge at the entrance to
this Daurian pika burrow. Numerous
droppings were present in the
immediate vicinity.

continues to inhabit screes even when their external appearance has completely changed. The development of these screes is described by N. A. Avrorin in his work on forest types of the Altai Mountains and is quoted by Ognev: "Screes result at first from eolian disintegration of rocks. Such 'young' and energetically-growing screes are mobile and overgrown with lichens. Neither mosses nor flowering plants can exist in them. In the second stages the screes become 'quiescent,' the stones losing their mobility. Such screes are covered with moss and some flowering plants (*Sedum hybridum*). Distintegrating rock particles reach the lower margin of the scree more rarely and vegetation is thus more intensive there. The following plants can be found at the periphery of the screes: currant (*Ribes nigrum, R. atropurpureum*), gooseberry (*Ribes grossularia*), very fragrant and sweet raspberry (*Rubus melanolasius*), etc.

"Later screes become densely overgrown with *Caragana arborescens* [the Siberian peashrub], *Lonicera caerulea, L. microphylla, Spiraea chamaedryfolia, Berberis siberica*, etc. The afforestation of the 'old' scree takes place under the shelter of these shrubs.

"According to A. M. Koslov, pikas do not leave screes, even when screes of the first type become gradually transformed into mountain forest regions."

In central Asia a large alpine pika colony was found on the east coast of Lake Ity-Kul by V. V. Dmitriev who transmitted his observations to Professor Ognev. There the screes had completely lost their primitive character. There was no alluvial soil and the stones and rocks were covered with moss. The pikas lived in burrows whose entrances were covered with green moss. Large cedar groves interspersed with spruce grew on the screes which were on the north-facing slopes of the mountains. Rosemary and round-leaved birch occurred in thickets and provided the pikas with food.

Another Mongolian pika, referred to by Ognev as Price's pika (*Ochotona pricei*) and as Pallas' pika (*Ochotona pallasi*) by Ellerman and Morrison-Scott in their classification of Asiatic mammals, ranges from the desert to about 8,000 feet in the Altai Mountains and on the southern part of the Kazakhstan Plateau. It seems to be most abundant in rocks with deep passages and in residual rocky outcrops on the desert. The passages in the rocks are the result of erosion by the elements and provide the pikas with protection from the wind. Their burrows are either under rocks or very near to them. Although not common on rockless deserts, they occur in such situations at times and have their burrows under peashrubs. In some localities there is an overlap between this species and *Ochotona daurica*. The latter, however, tends to show an avoidance of rocky areas while Price's pika prefers rocks and may be found in areas where the Siberian ibex (*Capra siberica*) grazes.

An interesting custom of the Price's pika is the gathering of large heaps of rubble composed of camel and horse dung, stones, and pieces of vegetation near the entrance to their burrows. Sometimes these hillocks almost block the burrow entrances. It is believed that these piles of debris are used principally to block the wind and to prevent water from entering the burrows.

The small pika (*Ochotona pusilla*) ranges from south-central Siberia and eastern Kazakhstan west to the Ural Mountains of southeastern Europe. In the Pleistocene its range was much more extensive. Fossil remains have been found in Germany, France, Belgium, and the British Isles. Its habitat is quite varied and ranges from meadowland to thickets of wild rose, wild cherry, and other shrubs under which it burrows. It is fairly common around villages and in farmland.

From these descriptions of the various kinds of habitats occupied by Eurasian pikas, one can see the relative versatility exhibited by members of this genus, from forest dwellers to inhabitants of rocky alpine slopes. This, combined with their ability to subsist on a wide variety of food plants, could account for their success in the

The typical crouching position of a Daurian
pika as it pauses briefly along its runway.

rigorous climates of central and northern Asia. It is also easy to see how the progenitors of the North American pikas were able to cross the Bering Land Bridge in the Pleistocene and successfully invade North America.

Spring

WE HAVE NOW set the stage for the small mammal that is the subject of this book. The environment it inhabits, whether it be the rocky peaks of western North America or the vast desolate reaches of northern Asia, is a severe one for many months of the year. Let us consider how the inhabitants, both plant and animal, react as the days become longer and the earth warmer.

Winter Ends

The phenomena associated with spring start almost imperceptibly as winter comes to a close, and they are correlated with changing daylength. In the Northern Hemisphere this means a gradual increase of each day after the winter solstice in December. By the time of the vernal equinox in March, the periods of night and day are approximately equal. This progressive increase in the photoperiod

36

means that the earth is exposed to the warmth of the sun's rays for a slightly longer time each day. The increased heat gradually melts the snow and warms the soil. During the previous summer, myriads of seeds were produced by the various kinds of plant life in the community. Vast numbers were consumed by birds, mammals, and many other kinds of organisms. Some, however, were overlooked or were so hidden that they survived the onslaught. All winter they have been in or on the ground where the cover of snow protected them. With warmth and moisture now available, a change takes place.

A seed is not a simple structure. In many species, when it is formed on the parent plant, it develops an embryo within a protective covering. This embryo is a potential plant and has within or surrounding it a temporary food supply. When growth starts in the spring, the cotyledons, the embryonic leaves, begin to grow upward toward the surface of the ground; from the opposite end of the seed's axis the root begins to push downward. Growth at this time is dependent upon the stored food which consists of carbohydrates, fats, and proteins. Once the leaves emerge from the ground, the plants begin to produce their own food; the seedling is no longer dependent upon the embryonic stored food which is almost gone. Different seeds require different lengths of time to germinate. Consequently all species do not come up at the same time in the spring.

While the seeds of various annual and perennial plants are in the process of germinating after the snow melts, other plants, especially lilies, have passed the winter as bulbs. A bulb is really just a very short stem of a plant with a lot of fleshy basal leaves surrounding it in a series of concentric rings, such as is evident in a section of an onion. Food is stored in these thick leaves and, when the ground becomes moist and warm in spring, plants such as camas lilies, corn lilies, and wild onions begin their growth and push their stems and leaves above the ground. Other plants, especially perennial grasses,

Dense brush, consisting principally of
manzanita, huckleberry oak, and bitter cherry,
surrounds this pile of talus which houses a
pika colony at 6,500 feet elevation in the
central Sierra Nevada.

have survived the winter by means of underground root stocks that were dormant.

As the various kinds of herbaceous plants are bursting forth from seeds, bulbs, rootstocks, and other special devices that enabled them to survive winter, changes are rapidly occurring in larger forms of plant life. Deciduous trees and shrubs lost all their leaves the previous autumn. As spring approaches, buds located along and at the tips of the branches begin to swell. These buds are destined to give rise to leaves, flowers, and other stems or branches. Several weeks of warm weather will soon bring forth the leaves of aspen, alder, and dogwood. Before the willows leaf out, the catkins begin to appear. Each tree has its own sex; some bear male catkins that produce pollen, while others produce female catkins that will develop the seeds.

The process of photosynthesis begins in green plants after the plant has emerged from the soil. This is probably the most important chemical reaction on earth. It is the process of producing carbohydrates from carbon dioxide and water in the presence of chlorophyll and sunlight. Chlorophyll is the green coloring matter in the chloroplasts of plant cells and is a necessary catalyst for the bringing about of this reaction. Were it not for the remarkable ability of green plants to harness the sun's energy and produce organic food from simple inorganic substances, there would be no life on earth. In addition to producing carbohydrates, it provides certain materials needed to form amino acids which are the chief component of protein molecules. Vitamins are another product of plant life. The very process of photosynthesis itself removes carbon dioxide, eliminated from animals into the air, and returns oxygen, which is so vital to animal life.

While most plant life has been dormant all winter, certain animals, like the pika, have been active. Their source of energy has been plant material they had gathered the previous spring, summer, and

The snow which covered this south-facing
pika rock pile at about 6,500 feet elevation
in the Lake Tahoe region of central California
has all melted by the end of May.

fall. By late winter these stocks have been depleted and the resumption of photosynthesis and consequent plant growth is of vital importance.

Spring comes slowly at higher elevations, often weeks or even months after activities have started lower down. A favorite pika colony of mine is in a rocky slope at about 8,000 feet, several miles back of our Sierran cabin. One May 25 we climbed for hours to reach this spot, only to find it still under many feet of snow and the nearby lake frozen. It would be some weeks more before the rocky homes of these pikas would be exposed to the rays of the sun. A few miles away and 2,000 feet lower, pika colonies were snow-free and spring activity had begun.

Even though a heavy blanket of snow remains, some residents do not wait for it to melt. Rosy finches or leucostictes, those alpine relations of the house finch and purple finch, begin nesting before the neighboring pikas emerge. Their nests are made of moss and grass placed in a crack in a cliff or under an exposed rock in the talus. Much of their food at these high levels consists of insects swept up from below by air currents and deposited on the surface of the snow.

In the white bark and lodgepole pines adjacent to alpine rockslides near timberline, Clark's nutcrackers start their nesting activities very early. Their grating calls are familiar to the other inhabitants of the high mountains.

While alpine birds like rosy finches and Clark's nutcrackers seem to be ahead of pikas at high elevations, activities at lower levels are much more widespread. As the aspens begin to leaf out, sapsuckers are industriously constructing or, as is more often the case, reconstructing nest holes in their trunks. Unused nest holes are rapidly occupied by house wrens newly arrived from the south. Both indicate their territories in different ways, one by drumming, the other by song. As soon as the aspen leaves provide a sufficient cover, warbling

By June in the Sierra Nevada, corn lilies are
growing rapidly and the low herbaceous
vegetation provides cover and food for voles.

vireos will arrive and build their compact nests. These are made of moss and hang from a twig. As the male sings with seemingly endless energy, the female lays her tiny, white, lilac brown spotted eggs and begins her incubating duties.

The willows at these lower levels are not dwarfed like the alpine species next to the pika slides above timberline. They are large, bushy shrubs that line the small rushing streams coming down the mountain slopes or meandering through the meadows. By early June they are providing nesting sites for a variety of birds. The songs of white-crowned sparrows and Wilson's warblers are heard in willow thickets in nearly every mountain meadow. Both may nest in the branches or on the ground beneath. Adjacent to weedy growth in the meadow, the bubbling song of a Lincoln's sparrow may be heard.

As the grass in the mountain meadow renews its growth, the trails of voles become more and more evident. These little animals have been active all winter under the snow, but now new green growth is available. Their trails, from their burrows through the grass, are used day and night. The increased food supply enriched with vitamins seems to stimulate reproductive activity. Young are soon born and mature rapidly. By the time the females are four weeks old, they may become pregnant and have their own young three weeks later. Their high reproductive rate is necessary for survival, since they are preyed upon by many other animals. Their lives are short but active.

Pocket gophers have also been busy all winter and, to prove it, have left round cores of earth on the surface of the ground, even over rocks and small fallen logs. These cores were pushed up from subterranean tunnels during the continuation of their burrows through the winter snow. These above-ground tunnels in the snow enabled them to secure the bark of shrubs and trees for food in complete safety. Adjacent to pika colonies, it is likely that the two species may be competitors during the winter for the same kinds of food.

A talus inhabited by pikas in the Rocky
Mountains, Montana, in late June.

In the coniferous forests that clothe the mountain slopes and surround the meadows, spring is also bringing many changes. Pines, firs, hemlocks, cedars, and other conifers must reproduce like other plants. In spring, male and female cones are produced on the same tree. The staminate cones are small and papery, unlike the woody, scaled female cones which take two or three years to mature. When the staminate cones are ripe and open, the air is filled with yellow pollen falling on everything on the forest floor.

Many summer resident birds inhabit the evergreen forests, arriving as soon as the snow melts and food becomes available for the young soon to be produced. Warblers, vireos, flycatchers, tanagers, juncos, and others soon begin to outnumber the year-round residents. The song of the hermit thrush, a beautiful, wild, flutelike series of notes, fills the forest in the evening. Where there are banks and large boulders, one may be fortunate to hear the high, clear song of Townsend's solitaire. The male frequently selects a perch on the top of a tall dead tree on a fairly open slope. At the height of the breeding season, he may leave his singing perch and continue the song as he flies upward in a spiral course. Yellow-rumped warblers that were so widespread in the lowland valleys and along the coast during the winter months can be seen and heard almost throughout the coniferous forest. The males now have bright yellow rumps and throats in contrast to their black breasts and white bellies. While they sing to announce their territories, the females build their bulky nests of bark and pine needles fairly high up in the trees.

Occasionally, with luck, one will hear the far-reaching call of the pileated woodpecker, whose wingspread exceeds two feet. By careful approach, it may be possible to see this large bird, with its bright red head and pointed crest, perched on a tall dead snag. When it drums, it sounds like a lumberjack striking a log with a mallet. If it takes flight, the large white wing patches contrast conspicuously with its black body feathers. Other smaller woodpeckers are much

The earthen cores of pocket gophers'
above-ground winter activities remain after
the snow has melted.

more common in the forest. These include the hairy, white-headed, and three-toed species. Each plays a very important role in controlling forest insects, especially bark-dwelling types that become active as the weather warms up.

Woodpeckers serve another purpose in the avian community by providing nesting sites for secondary hole-nesting species such as the mountain bluebird, nuthatch, and violet green swallow. The bills of these birds are not adapted to chipping away the wood. Most of these nest sites are in standing dead trees. These may be an eyesore to the forester, but their presence is essential to many avian species, most of which are insect eaters. Their removal could be detrimental to the surrounding living trees by permitting an increase in the numbers of injurious insects.

As the songs of newly-arrived birds are heard everywhere in the pines and firs and the trees themselves are engaged in renewed activity which will ultimately lead to the production of cones, changes are occurring on the forest floor. Higher up the slopes, where many snowbanks are still to be found among the trees, there are fungi pushing up through their edges. This snowbank flora is very unique, and the species involved are uniquely adapted to this strange environment. The strands or webs of the fungus plants involved become active before the snow leaves the surface of the ground. Gradually they begin to form the fleshy fruiting bodies. As these grow, they melt the marginal snow where it is only an inch or two thick and emerge through it like little parasols or miniature cups. One of the more beautiful species is *Lyophyllum montanum*. The stems are about three inches long and the caps are one to two inches in diameter. All parts are a soft pale gray which makes them look like tiny ghosts against their white background. As soon as the snow melts around them, they stand out conspicuously against the dark moist soil. Another attractive snowbank fungus is entirely black and shaped like a tiny cup on a stalk about an inch or two long. At a distance it merely appears as a black spot on the edge of the snow.

As certain fungi fruit along the receding snow line as it ascends the mountain slopes, others wait until the earth has warmed up. By the time the pines begin to drop their pollen, the beautiful green-tinged orange cups of the *Calocypha fulgens* are abundant on the forest floor. Soon after emergence, their surface becomes sprinkled with yellow pollen. Larger gilled fungi, such as *Russula brevipes*, push up great mounds of needles which give away their presence beneath. This particular species is very common in spring as well as autumn in the mountains of western North America. Its large size and pure white color with just a tint of blue where the gills meet the stem make it most attractive. In parts of Europe, this, or the closely related *Russula delica*, are pickled in salt and preserved in barrels for use in cooking during the year.

All over the Northern Hemisphere, May is known as the month for morels. These May mushrooms have been sought for centuries by gourmets. One never divulges, even to close friends, a special collecting site. In the Sierra Nevada, the Cascades, and the Rocky Mountains, one searches the floor of forests of white fir, Douglas fir, ponderosa pine, and spruce for these delectable fungi. Their caps look like miniature pine cones and are often difficult to distinguish at a distance. If tobacco brush or snowbush, both species of the genus *Ceanothus*, are present, they may be hidden under their branches. Squirrels, deer, and other animals besides man search them out in the spring. These and a number of other fungi fruit in the spring in the mountains of the West, although most species make their appearance in autumn.

Fungi belong to a group of plants that lack chlorophyll and cannot produce their own food, hence they must feed on living or dead organic matter. However, they are not the only plants to live this way. Spring has not progressed very far before the brilliant stalks of the snowplant begin pushing up among the litter of conifer needles like giant red asparagus tips. As they grow, the flowers, stems, and bracts, all red, depend entirely on decaying humus in the soil. This strange species is a member of the wintergreen family which contains certain other saprophytic plants and root parasites. Pinedrops is another saprophyte that often comes up near snowplants. Its stalks are a dark purple brown and the leaves are scalelike. Nodding flowers of red to white are borne along the stem. This species secures its food from the roots of living conifers rather than from the humus.

Where snowplants and pinedrops grow, one may often find ridges along the surface of the moist ground in late spring. These represent the foraging tunnels of moles. Moles are small mammals, related to shrews, that are adapted to a completely subterranean life. During the winter they forage deep for earthworms and various other small invertebrate animals. As the earthworms come toward the surface in the spring, moles forage for them under the litter. Occasionally there will be a large mound of earth on the surface where a mole has pushed soil up from the deep tunnels in which it lives when not searching for food.

Most rocky slopes below timberline where pikas may live are adjacent to thickets of brush. Such kinds of vegetation grow in these partly rocky places where trees find difficulty in surviving. As spring arrives, various species of manzanita, bitter cherry, and snowbush come into bloom. Their fragrance fills the air and myriads of insects come to feed on their nectar and pollen. New avian arrivals, restricted to this kind of habitat, take up residency and begin their nesting. Fox sparrows sing loud and clear from various posts, each male announcing its newly established territory to other males in the vicinity.

Less conspicuous than the fox sparrows but equally defensive are the green-tailed towhees, relatives of the lowland rufous-sided and brown towhees and similarly fond of brushy cover. From the nearby

The golden-mantled ground squirrel is a
common associate of the pika in rockslides.

rocks one may hear the beautiful liquid notes of the canyon wren descending the scale and becoming slower and slower toward the end. They are rather rare in the high mountains but, where they do occur, it is often in and adjacent to a rockslide where pikas may be found.

General Behavior

Spring means many things in the life of a pika. No longer must it depend on dry hay gathered and stored the previous autumn or on such living vegetation as can be obtained by tunneling under the snow. New fresh growths of herbs are emerging from the ground adjacent to the rocks, and fresh green buds are appearing on the shrubs. Pikas are herbivores and avail themselves of many kinds of plants for food. In fact, judging from the contents of their haypiles, nearly every kind of vegetation within their reach is taken by our North American species.

As spring starts there is considerable competition for newly sprouting herbs, as well as the buds and leaves of various shrubs. In many parts of western North America, marmots are common inhabitants of the pikas' rockpiles, and both feed on many of the same species while plant life is still sparse. Occasionally a sow bear, just recently out of hibernation, will arrive on a favorable slope next to a talus. She may even have denned up during the winter under some of the larger boulders where her cubs were born. The cubs are now old enough to forage with her, and the same vegetation sought by the pikas and the marmots is attractive to these omnivores. Pikas, too, would provide the female and her cubs with choice morsels of food if they could be captured. But the chance of this happening to these alert little animals is very slim.

Until new seeds are formed later on in summer, the various kinds of ground squirrels and chipmunks associated with rockslides must

In the spring, just after the snow has melted, pikas are extremely wary and alert to any unusual sounds or movements.

(*Photograph by Douglas B. Herr*)

feed on fresh vegetation of one sort or another. Some of this is provided by the nearby herbaceous growth. As summer approaches, food plants become more abundant and competition for them between species is reduced.

Pikas are much more wary in the spring than later in the year. An animal that has been living for months in a hidden world beneath a deep protective covering of snow, in intense silence, with the absence of movement except by members of its own kind, is going to be wary on emergence in the spring. In this new situation leaves are rustling in the wind, nesting birds can be heard singing, and other small mammals, from the chipmunk to the marmot, are carrying on their activities about the talus. Furthermore, the absence of snow means the loss of protection from attack by certain avian and mammalian predators. To secure food it is necessary to venture into the open, away from the protecting rocks. Caution is required until familiarity with this new environment is once again acquired.

Pikas are alert to both sound and movement. No matter how quietly you approach a rockslide inhabited by these little animals, a sentinel will detect you and give a series of warning calls. The call may be a single bark, but more often consists of two calls in close succession. Sometimes as many as ten consecutive barks are given at about half-second intervals. There are also marked geographic differences in the calls of pikas. In the Sierra Nevada of California the bark is sharp and rather rasping, whereas in the Rocky Mountains it is much softer and more like the bleat of a lamb. This tends to support the view formerly held that southern pikas in these two regions are specifically distinct.

Warning calls are usually given from a large rock which slopes backward rather than downhill. The calling individual therefore has a broad view of the slope below and, if further alarmed, can move backward into a crevice. Very often the rock or slab from which a

Long after the snow has melted in late spring
near the shore of Lake Tahoe it remains
in patches on the higher slopes.

warning call is given has another large rock overhanging it, giving further protection to the sentinel. Several pikas may call from different parts of a large rockslide. When disturbed, vocalization may continue from deep within a rock pile.

Loukashkin has described the call of the Daurian pika in Manchuria as a very musical series of notes that are birdlike in quality. They begin high and progressively descend the scale. These calls are given most often just after daybreak and again after sunset. Professor S. I. Ognev, in his monumental work, *Mammals of the U.S.S.R. and Adjacent Countries*, similarly describes the call of the Daurian pika as a long, rolling trill gradually subsiding and becoming weaker at the end, like the warble of the pipit (*Anthus trivialis*).

The call of the northern pika (*Ochotona hyperborea*) is described by Loukashkin as a very loud, sharp, monotonous whistle. Ognev says that the call of one individual is echoed by others if danger is imminent and, after they retreat to the safety of their burrows, the calls are continued for some time and then gradually decrease. On emerging again, they usually call fifteen to thirty times.

Pikas react differently to different kinds of predators. A hawk flying overhead instantly evokes warning barks. Similarly, the approach of a medium-sized or large mammalian carnivore such as the pine marten or coyote produces warning barks. A small enemy like a weasel does not. The weasel, because of its size, can enter all the crevices and passageways the pika can; therefore, a quiet retreat is advantageous.

Vocalization serves not only to warn other members of a colony of impending danger, but also to advertise territory. Studies on two Himalayan species of pikas, *Ochotona macrotis* and *O. royalei*, by Takeo Kawamichi have shown a weak development of voice. This seems to be correlated with a lack of haypiles. American pikas have a highly developed haypile habit which is associated with strong territoriality, especially in late summer and fall. It is then that vocalization functions to announce an individual's territory and represents an aggressive sound against a potential invader.

Pikas are primarily diurnal animals, most active during the morning and late afternoon hours, but there may be some activity at night. The northern pika in Asia (*O. hyperborea*) is said to be most active at dawn and in the evening. During the middle of the day, if it is warm, most of their time will be spent under rocks or in burrows; but if it is cool they will continue their activities. Inclement weather such as rain or snow restricts their activities. I once watched a rockslide inhabited by a colony of pikas in Montana for an hour during a moderate rain and failed to see or hear a single individual.

Although pikas are active in the open only during daylight hours, they may call frequently during the night. On several occasions, when I have camped next to a rockslide inhabited by pikas, I have heard their call throughout the night. In late June one year, my wife and I camped near two rockslides inhabited by these animals. We heard their call notes many times during the night, and by 7:30 the next morning, individuals were industriously gathering food on the adjacent slopes. Nocturnal calling has also been noted in most of the Asiatic species of pikas.

Both American and Asiatic species of pikas have definite trails that they follow to and from their feeding areas. In North America these are seen most often leading out from the periphery of rockslides. They may extend twenty to thirty yards from the protection of the rocks. In Outer Mongolia I found areas in which colonies of Daurian pikas lived to be a maze of runways. Some led from one burrow entrance to another, while others went to feeding grounds or even to the edge of a creek. These trails were three to four inches in width and very obvious in the lush vegetation. The animals moved

Winter lingers longer on pika rockslides
near timberline. Deciduous trees do not
leaf out until it is summer lower down.

Black bears emerge from hibernation in the
spring hungry for both plant and animal food.

very rapidly along them and, from the side, were difficult to see unless they stood on their hind legs. Sometimes piles of debris cleaned out from a burrow were found along the side of a trail close to the burrow entrance. Haypiles were also situated along the sides of these trails.

Wherever there are pikas, their droppings are very evident. The small, dry, round pellets remind one of diminutive rabbit droppings. American pikas most often deposit their droppings at specific places in their rock piles. These are often in the open, but excavation of rocks on slopes where pikas live have shown that these places for defecation may also be deep under the rocks. It is probable that the latter sites are used primarily in winter.

In Outer Mongolia the droppings of the Daurian pikas are found along their trails, but they are most concentrated near the burrow entrance. The pellets are very similar to those of North American species.

Pikas, like hares and rabbits, are coprophagous, that is, they will eat their own droppings. The practice of coprophagy is believed to serve a nutritional demand for vitamin B. Substances containing this vitamin are formed in the caecum of lagomorphs and voided without being absorbed by the body. By eating their own pellets, a nutritional deficiency is prevented. Ryoichi Haga, in his study of Japanese pikas in captivity, found that the fresh fecal pellets are deep green and about three to four millimeters in diameter. They are voided mostly during the daytime. The second type of pellet, eliminated at night, is elongate rather than spherical, and measures about three by twenty to thirty millimeters. The night feces are viscous and encased in a gelatinous substance, while the day pellets are hard and friable.

Urine also is usually deposited at specific places, often near haypiles or dens. The urine is very dark, but when the same rock is used for many years the encrustations become white.

Pikas usually deposit their droppings in
very definite localities.

Reproduction

For most animals species, reproduction is a most important spring activity. The increased daylength stimulates gonadal activity. Food becomes abundant with plants starting the chain and the herbivores feeding on the new-grown vegetation. In many species this is the time when aggressive territorial behavior becomes most evident. This behavior is thought to perform several different functions, such as providing nesting sites and food for the young, a means of limiting the population to the carrying capacity of the environment, protection for the young against other members of the same species, and, in some instances, a means of strengthening the sexual bond between members of a mated pair. The pikas reverse this situation found in so many herbivores. Territoriality and aggressiveness are at their lowest in the spring when reproduction begins. Conflicts between individuals of either sex are rare at this time of year, a rather unique situation for most higher vertebrates. As the season progresses and the young are reared, territorial behavior begins to appear, reaching peak aggressive and possessive behavior in late summer and fall, after the reproduction period.

The peak of the breeding season in North America is reached in May and early June. Since females born the previous spring and summer are sexually mature, all of the females in a colony are potentially capable of bearing young. Furthermore, females are receptive to males again right after they bear their first litter in the spring, a trait characteristic of other members of the order Lagomorpha. The gestation period in the pika is about thirty days, so the female may have her second litter of the season by early July. The number of young in a litter generally ranges from two to four in *Ochotona princeps*—a relatively high fertility rate.

Nevertheless, many factors reduce the potentially high offspring population. Most pikas live in regions where weather conditions can

At 9,000 feet, toward the end of May, most pika colonies are still snow-bound in the high Sierra Nevada.

suddenly become very severe in the late spring, and occasionally this adverse weather results in the loss of the first litter. Under unfavorable environmental pressures, females may resorb their embryos. Among second litters the mortality rate is usually higher than for the first-born of the year.

Some of the Asiatic pikas have an even higher fertility rate than those in western America. The alpine pika is reported to produce four to six young per litter. In his book, Professor Ognev quotes Soviet scientist B. A. Kuznetsov as having observed the young of the first litter out and living in separate burrows by late June. At the same time, young of the second litter were being suckled and were about the size of a vole (meadow mouse).

The Daurian pika definitely seems to have at least two litters each summer. Members of the American Museum's Asiatic Expedition captured young animals about half-grown in northern Mongolia on May 18 and 19, while Ognev reports that members of A. N. Formozov's expedition to Central Asia found young individuals throughout the summer. One female taken on August 2 had five young ready for birth, and another female, captured on September 2, contained five embryos and was accompanied by three half-grown young. In this instance one would suspect that she was pregnant for the third time that summer.

There is little or no special courtship behavior known among pikas. Aggression and territorial behavior are at their lowest during the early part of the reproductive season. At this time males engage in greater wandering than later in the season, and males and females may occupy, for brief periods, the same territory. The care of the young, as in hares and rabbits, is confined to the female.

Newborn pikas are very lightly furred and have their ears and eyes closed. R. Haga, who studied the northern pika in captivity in Japan, found the upper and lower incisors to be slightly erupted at this time. By the sixth day after birth the molars are visible but

Even though it is late spring, snow still covers a rockslide inhabited by a number of pikas.

have not yet erupted. When eight days old, the young can walk, although unsteadily, and begin to call. Haga reports that a young pika that weighed 60 grams on July 12 when captured had a weight of 120 grams, which is that of an adult, on August 9. It would appear from such evidence that full size is attained at an age of forty to fifty days, which is a remarkably rapid rate of growth. This, of course, is necessary in an animal that is on its own in a region of very severe winter climate. Before the onset of that season, young born in the summer must establish territories and stockpile an adequate food supply to last until the following spring.

Summer

As SUMMER GRADUALLY SUCCEEDS SPRING, the general environment of the pika in the mountains of western North America undergoes further change. Most of the rockslides at or above timberline are now free of snow, especially those on south-facing slopes. On the patches of soil interspersed among the rocks, alpine flowers are beginning to appear. The western pasque flower, which really has no petals but possesses large, showy white sepals, is among the more conspicuous plants. Growing out from crevices in the rocks where it seems impossible that anything could find sustenance are the fronds of the rock brake. This fern has two kinds of leaves, those that bear spores and those that are sterile. In slightly clearer areas where small rivulets rush down as a network of miniature channels, the bright yellow flowers of the glacier lilies or, as they are commonly known, dogtooth violets, create a splash of color.

Alpine meadows in glacial cirques, sometimes partly encircled by talus, are coming into full flower as summer progresses. Around the rocky margins and along small streams of snow water both the white and beautiful rose purple mountain heathers are attaining full bloom. The generic name of the former is *Cassiope*, who, in Greek mythology, was set among the stars as a constellation. The mountain heather is named *Phyllodoce* after a Greek nymph. It reminds one very much of the heathers that abound in the Scottish highlands.

Out in the meadows themselves many other flowers are blooming. The alpine lungwort, with its blue flowers, contrasts with the yellow alpine buttercup. Probably the most typical flowers of the small meadows at or above timberline are the gentians. They are regarded as among the most beautiful of montane species. The long, funnel-shaped corollas of some are a very deep blue. Others are greenish white with darker spots inside. In some, the margins of the petals are finely fringed.

The alpine willow is perhaps a remnant of the glacial periods of the Pleistocene. It is the counterpart in our high southern mountains of the arctic willow in the northern tundra. Looking more like a small creeping shrub, its shoots attain a height of only one to six inches. The male and female catkins it bears, each on a different plant, are taller than the diminutive plant itself.

A little farther down the slopes among hemlocks, white pines, and tamaracks, the small Labrador tea bushes are laden with umbels of white flowers. They too are members of the heath or heather family. The currants and gooseberries which are all members of the genus *Ribes* are nearly finished flowering and soon their fruits will be available to the many birds and mammals. The forest floor of the higher parts of the Rocky Mountains is covered at this season with Canadian dogwood, whose beautiful white flowers are really bracts or modified leaves surrounding a head of minute true flowers.

The larger meadows lower down, at middle elevation, now have corn lilies in full bloom. Where they are absent there may be large patches of pink elephant's head, especially where moist. On the hill-sides and ridges, great plumes of bear grass may be seen from a considerable distance. This is really not a grass but a member of the lily family that looks somewhat like miniature pampas grass and may attain a height of six feet when mature. Various American Indian tribes used its bulbs for food and the fibers in the leaves for weaving.

Among the willows bordering the meadow many shade-loving plants are now coming into bloom. The bright orange flowers with black spots belonging to the alpine lily have just opened. They are re-garded as choice morsels by deer, so many of the buds have been nipped. Only those that are well camouflaged have survived. Mingled with them are the spikes of the monkshood whose blue flowers closely resemble the nearly-related delphiniums. The monks-hood belongs to the genus *Aconitum* and is a source of drug. Much less conspicuous and often hidden in the undergrowth is Solomon's seal whose small white flowers are in the form of a plumelike raceme.

This is also the time of year for mountain orchids. The rein orchid, common in the higher mountains, belongs to the genus *Habenaria* which comes from the Latin *habena*, meaning the rein of a horse. Their flowers have a spur that is shaped like a rein. These plants favor moist, shaded places around the edges of mountain meadows.

With the arrival of summer most birds are either well into their nesting activities or have already finished them. By late June the ventriloquial hooting of the male blue grouse is no longer heard. The female has completed incubation and is herding her flock of chicks through the forest, trying to protect them from potential enemies. Sapsuckers and woodpeckers have nearly finished their territorial drumming on the trunks of trees and snags. Most of the small birds are actively feeding young that are still in the nest or have just been fledged but are not yet old enough to take care of

By late June, bull elk have started their
antler growth.

themselves. Insect food is now abundant and feeding is interrupted only by an occasional thunderstorm.

Mule deer does can occasionally be seen with their fawns. These still have their white spots, allowing them to blend with their background when lying quietly on the ground. The bucks are higher up on the ridges, their new antlers growing rapidly. It will not be long before the living covering of velvet dies and will be rubbed off. This must occur before the rutting season starts in the fall. In the Rocky Mountains, the elk have migrated upward to the high country where they will stay until the snows of autumn force them down. They are much more gregarious than deer. The females that have borne calves in May and June keep to themselves for a while, but soon the groups become larger and many immature males join them. The bulls will stay apart until their antlers grow and will be ready to stake out territories and fight for harems of females before the winter sets in.

Various members of the squirrel family are ending the reproductive season. The young are going out on their own and eagerly searching for food. If they are to survive, they must attain full growth before it is time to hibernate in the fall. Mountain meadows nearly everywhere are inhabited by small ground squirrels commonly known as picket-pins. This term has been applied to them because of the upright position they assume when on the alert. Standing on the soles of their hind feet with the body vertical and the front legs pressed against the belly, they utter a series of shrill notes when disturbed. Each has its own burrow system into which it scurries in time of danger. They are strictly ground dwellers and rarely venture into rocky situations.

Where rocks are present around these mountain meadows there are likely to be golden-mantled ground squirrels. This is a species that does not venture out into open, picket-pin country. It prefers boulder-strewn areas, often in the conifers and rocks where it is a close associate of the pika. Summer activities of all these ground squirrels are very much alike although their food is quite different. The picket-pin depends largely upon various grasses. Golden-mantled ground squirrels (*Citellus lateralis*) are primarily seed eaters. They were formerly classified in the genus *Callospermophilus* which, when translated, means beautiful seed lover. Indeed this is our most colorful North American ground squirrel. They have a white stripe, bordered with black, on either side of the body, and the head, neck, and shoulders are a bright cinnamon or russet brown color.

Marmots, like other members of the squirrel family in the high mountains, have their young early in the summer. The young, when they emerge from burrows along the margins of alpine meadows or from deep in rockslides, begin feeding almost immediately. There is no lengthy childhood nor time for play. Hibernation will begin in late August or early September when summer is barely over. During the few weeks available they must build up their body weight and accumulate sufficient fat to tide them through the long winter. Their food consists largely of grasses and the leaves and stems of various herbs and shrubs.

Summer represents a time of maturity for most kinds of plant and animal life. The blossoms of spring have turned into fruits, nuts, berries, and seeds which will not only insure the perpetuation of the species, but provide food for the many kinds of animals. It is a time when the cones are ripening and when the young of various animals are growing up. Summer comes between the reproductive season of spring and the time when life in the higher mountains prepares for the long winter to come. The arrival of summer has another effect upon the pika.

Territory

With the gradual passing of spring, behavioral changes take place among pikas, whether they live in a Sierran rockslide or high in a

Alpine habitat of pikas resulting from the
fracturing of surface granite by the elements
since the Pleistocene. The margin of this
small meadow was used for foraging
in late summer.

Mongolian valley. The tacit permission for an intruder to enter another's territory is replaced by open aggression toward the offender. The reproductive activities begin to wane but do not cease entirely. The new young, out in the sunshine for the first time, become restless, as does the female parent. She soon forces them to leave and search for homes of their own while she is still preparing for her second litter, if they have not yet been born.

Associated with the developing territorial behavior, which may include not only defense of the home area but also the adjacent feeding grounds, is the start of haymaking, the gathering of food for winter use. By autumn this will be the major daily activity. A number of studies have been made in recent years on the territorial behavior of *Ochotona princeps* in the Rocky Mountains. Lewis M. Lutton found that, in Colorado, territorial behavior started at the beginning of July when the chasing of one individual by another occurred frequently. This is the time when haypiling begins. By mid-July chases were observed at least once an hour and more definite territorial boundaries became noticeable. Kawamichi, studying pikas in the same state, found extensive overlaps in territories resulting in frequent encounters. In such instances the invader, male or female, enters a neighbor's territory. If detected, the occupant approaches the intruder. This usually results in the intruder being chased. When they enter the intruder's territory, a reversal takes place and the original invader now goes after the occupant that formerly chased it. Expulsion is not always successful because of dominance and subdominance, especially in males. Males frequently invade the territory of other males as well as females. While males are sometimes tolerated in territories of females, especially during the breeding season, the degree of dominance is clearly recognizable when one adult male enters the territory of another adult male.

The social relationship of females to one another is one of repul-

Alpine habitat of pikas in late summer in the
south central Sierra Nevada. Isberg Peak in
the distance is 11,600 feet high.

sion. They do not tolerate one another and avoid wherever possible having bordering territories. They do, however, show a delayed encounter response to invading males. Females likewise are dominant over juveniles and rebuke young individuals that enter their territory. There is a difference in aggression between juvenile males and juvenile females. Juvenile males establish their territories more easily. Many times, however, juveniles establish territories early in the summer, before adult aggression increases, and are subsequently routed by the adults later in the season.

There are many occasions where one pika enters the territory of another without being detected. The terrain in which they live does not lend itself easily to detecting an invader. Large rocks and deep crevices make it very difficult for a small terrestrial mammal to oversee its fairly extensive property; pikas are occupied with other duties most of the time. Intruders rarely announce themselves, so many invasions go unnoticed by the owner. Kawamichi observed 208 invasions of which only 97 were detected by the owner.

Dominance and the defense of territory in summer is very important for autumn activities when vital food must be harvested and stored for winter use. Territories are not only announced by vocal utterance, but seem to be marked by scent. Cheek rubbing by individuals on rocks around their boundaries has been observed by many persons. This would seem to be one method of providing information on ownership. The use of cheek gland secretions is employed by many mammals, including house cats, to announce territory. It is not evident, however, that this scent is necessarily a warning. Elmer B. Harvey and Lauren E. Rosenberg made a study of the apocrine glands, skin glands that exude a secretion, present in the posterior cheek region of pikas. In these animals the cheek glands seem to be most active during the breeding season. The rubbing off of the secretion around the territories may provide information to members of the opposite sex.

Pikas use particular rocks for urine deposition, which is another means of announcing ownership. Observations made by Lawrence Kilham indicate that pellet deposits may be another marking method. He observed that haypiles were placed where the animals left their droppings and further noted that on one occasion a pika rose on its hind legs and voided urine on the haypile.

Territory and home range are not synonymous terms, so one must distinguish between the two. The home range refers to the entire range in which an animal moves, whereas territory is the area that is defended by the occupant. Home ranges frequently overlap. With pikas, the overlapping areas are in the feeding grounds. Where meadowland adjoins a talus inhabited by pikas, the territory in the talus where the nest site and the haypiles are located is vigorously defended against any intruder discovered from summer on through autumn. The feeding and harvesting area in the adjacent meadow may be an area of overlap where much less aggression is shown. However, if there is too extensive an overlap in the home range there may be frequent encounters.

Haga gives thirty meters as the average diameter of the home range of the Japanese pika. In Colorado, Kilham estimates that the pika population in suitable rockslides is about five individuals per acre. This is similar to the findings of David P. Barash in Montana, where he found territorial centers separated by twenty-five to thirty meters.

Associates

Pikas have a number of rodent associates that occupy the same general type of habitat. Some are competitors for food while others are not. Some give warning calls; these are seemingly recognized and taken advantage of by pikas and thereby are distinctly beneficial.

In western North America the most conspicuous inhabitants of

Pikas and yellow-bellied marmots were
common in these masses of granite slabs
above timberline. This is a south-facing slope
at 10,600 feet elevation in the central
Sierra Nevada.

rockslides in the higher mountains are yellow-bellied marmots (*Marmota flaviventris*). This is a member of the same genus as the groundhog of eastern North America. Also associated with rock-slides, but more northern in distribution, is the hoary marmot (*Marmota caligata*). Marmots are the largest members of the squirrel family on this continent, having stocky bodies about two feet long with short legs and tail. The yellow-bellied marmot is less restricted to rockslides than the pika, living along the edge of mountain meadows and even in partially open areas in coniferous forests. However, there are few rockslides in the high Sierra Nevada, Cascades, or Rocky Mountains that do not have this species as a resident. The name whistler is often used for this animal because when it suspects danger its alarm note is a loud whistle. All residents of the rockslide know the significance of this call.

Marmots, unlike pikas, hibernate during the winter. In the fall they accumulate a large amount of body fat which will act as fuel during the long winter months when they sleep, deep in their dens, with lowered body temperature, slow respiration and pulse, and a cessation of most other body functions. They go into hibernation rather early in the fall while food is still abundant and before the snows come. This is the time when pikas are doing their harvesting. As a result, there is no competition for food between the two species from September until the following March when the marmot emerges. Its early spring appearance may be at a time when there is still much snow on the slopes, so much so that pikas are still undercover. The breeding season starts immediately, and the young are born after a gestation period of one month. By the time the snow melts and new green vegetation begins to sprout on adjacent slopes or meadows, there is some competition between the two species for food.

In the summer, many marmots go into estivation, summer dormancy, for a while. Harold E. Broadbooks found that pikas in the high Cascades of Washington gathered the dried droppings of the marmots at this time and stored them in their haypiles, perhaps to gain some of the food value remaining from plants eaten by the larger animals.

During their periods of activity, marmots spend hours lying on flat rocks in the sun. From such vantage points they have an opportunity to watch for their enemies—the eagle, hawk, marten, coyote, fox, and bobcat—which are also enemies of pikas. If one of these predators is detected, the warning whistle is given before the lookout dives into the rocks for protection.

There is a somewhat similar relationship in some Asian areas between the pika and the Asiatic marmot, which is called the bobak or tarbagan (*Marmota bobak*). In Mongolia, this species often inhabits the same area as the Daurian pika and feeds on many of the same plants in spring and summer. Early hibernation, however, eliminates the food competition between the two species at a harvest time most critical for the pika.

In western North America the member of the squirrel family most commonly found in rockslides with pikas is the golden-mantled ground squirrel (*Citellus lateralis*). This is the most abundant and widely distributed ground squirrel in mountainous areas. Although also common in boulder-covered openings in the forest and along the edges of alpine meadows where their burrows are usually under large rocks, there are few pika slides that are not inhabited by this beautiful striped squirrel. When watching for pikas, one is apt to see golden-mantled ground squirrels first. The two species are nearly similar in size and both clamber over the rocks. Unlike many kinds of ground squirrels, the golden mantle is notably silent, only occasionally giving a high-pitched call note when danger is suspected.

Pikas note the danger calls of ground squirrels just as they do the marmot's or that of the red squirrel or chickaree in a nearby

In mid-summer, Columbian ground squirrels
are competing with pikas for food in many
parts of the Rocky Mountains.

conifer forest. Golden-mantled ground squirrels go into hibernation deep underground from about the beginning of October until the latter part of April. It is not likely that there is any significant competition for food between the two species, as the ground squirrel is primarily a seed eater. They consume the seeds of many plants, including conifers. Pikas live mostly on the stems, leaves, and bark of plants.

In parts of the northern Rocky Mountains, the Columbian ground squirrel (*Citellus columbianus*) may also be found in or close to areas inhabited by pikas, but they are less restricted to rocks than the golden-mantled species. This is the ground squirrel most often seen in Glacier and Jasper national parks.

All of the mammalian associates of the pikas mentioned so far are diurnal species that spend a number of months during the year in hibernation. One of the most widespread and common non-hibernating mammals that occurs in rockslides along with pikas in western North America is the bushy-tailed wood rat (*Neotoma cinerea*). The terms pack rat and trade rat are often used for this and other species of the genus *Neotoma*. This is because of their habit of gathering sticks and other materials which they keep adding to their houses whether they be under rocks, in cliff crevices, or under a deserted mountain cabin. Consequently, when not feeding, much of their night is spent in carrying or packing twigs and other objects in their mouths. They are also attracted to bright, shiny objects. People camping in the mountains near these animals sometimes find, on awakening, that a knife, spoon, or some other small tool is missing and in its place a twig. A trade is thus effected by the little nocturnal visitor. More serious are occasions when more valuable objects, such as watches and rings, are taken in the trade.

The food of bushy-tailed wood rats consists of berries, fruits, nuts, and even the bark of plants. A few of these items may bring them into competition with the pikas inhabiting the same rockslides. Since the wood rats are active all year round, as far as known, there may well be greater competition in winter when food is at a premium. Whether or not the rats invade the stored food of the small lagomorphs during this season is not known.

There are a few other non-carnivorous mammals that play significant roles in the lives of pikas. Chipmunks of the genus *Eutamias* are often found around or living in the edges of rockslides. However, they are primarily seed eaters and do not come into competition with pikas for food. Their warning calls, though, are apt to be heeded, and they in turn probably take advantage of the warning calls of pikas.

Wherever there are rockslides close to coniferous forests in western North America, one is likely to find porcupines (*Erithizon dorsatum*). Their large oval droppings among the rocks somewhat resemble those of the marmot but are usually slightly curved. While porcupines and pikas may occur together, they in no way compete with one another. The larger animals are too big to fit into crevices occupied by the pikas. Furthermore, their principal food consists of the soft, growing layer of coniferous trees just beneath the outer bark. The terminal twigs of various pines and, to a lesser extent, firs are usually selected. Non-coniferous trees such as alder and willow, as well as certain shrubs, may provide food in some regions where conifers are scarce or absent, but such vegetation is not important to pikas.

Broadbooks, in his description of the associates of the northern pika (*Ochotona collaris*) on Mt. McKinley, mentions that the hoary marmot (*Marmota caligata*) lived in the same rockslides and, just adjacent, arctic ground squirrels (*Citellus undulatus*) were to be found. Since the vegetation on the windswept slopes next to these slides is rather uniformly covered by plants only a few inches high, there probably is some competition for food. Another vertebrate inhabitant of some of the rockslides is the rock ptarmigan (*Lagopus mutus*), which depends on vegetation during much of the year.

Loukashkin mentions quite a list of small mammals which he found making use of the paths, tunnels, and burrows of the Daurian pika (*Ochotona daurica*) in northern Manchuria. These included the long-eared jerboa (*Allactaga mongolica*), the hamster (*Cricetulus furunculus*), and a number of small mouselike rodents. In the Great Khingan Range he trapped red-backed mice (*Clethrionomys rutilus*) and two species of field mice (*Apodemus major* and *A. mantchurica*) in the runways of the northern pika (*Ochotona hyperborea*).

Enemies

Like most other small herbivores, pikas have many enemies. Among mammals it is likely that there is much predation on these animals by members of the weasel family, which includes not only the various species of weasels but also the pine marten and wolverine in North America, and the sable, kolinsky, and yellow-throated marten in Asia. In the Sierra Nevada, the Cascades, and Rocky Mountains, the long-tailed weasel (*Mustela frenata*) is commonly seen hunting in talus. This is a species of very wide range, occurring from Canada to southern South America. It is found in the boreal forests of the north, the desert, and the tropics. Weasels are extremely powerful for their size and sometimes seem to kill for sheer pleasure.

On several occasions, while sitting quietly along the edge of a rockslide in the high Sierra, I have watched weasels hunting. They concentrate intensely on their prey, and once a weasel has set out on the trail of a pika, it is not likely to be easily diverted. Probably following largely by scent, it moves over and under rocks seemingly with a definite purpose. From a higher vantage point I have been able to see other pikas who do not distract the smaller predator from his selected victim, who usually seems to keep well ahead of the enemy. I have never been able to find out how these chases end, but I would suspect the weasel often wins.

In the higher mountains, where weasels and pikas both occur, the weasel has two coat colors. In the fall of the year the brown summer pelage which blends well with the color of the ground is shed and replaced by a white coat. This is an adaptation that enables it to approach its prey more easily in winter when the environment is snow-covered. Since weasels are active all winter and some remain within the protection of rockslides during at least a part of this season, they are probably year-round enemies with which pikas must contend. In the spring, as the snow melts, the weasel undergoes another molt in which the white pelage is replaced by the brown one of summer.

This change in coat color is not unique to the weasel, but occurs in other mammals such as the varying hare. The hare, however, assumes a white coat in winter so that it is less easily seen by its many enemies. We find similar color changes in some birds such as the ptarmigan in which the fall molt results in a white winter plumage and the spring molt results in a brown plumage. As in the varying hare, this is an adaptation that enables the individual to better blend with its environment and thereby have a greater chance to elude its enemies.

The changes in coat color in the hare and weasel seem to be regulated by the length of daylight and perhaps activity. By subjecting varying hares to daily periods of artificial light equal to that of summer months, they soon become physiologically brown, and if a patch of white winter fur is pulled out, new incoming hairs will be brown. Conversely, if hares in summer are given only a few hours of illumination daily, they will become physiologically white and new hair growing in a plucked area on the body will come in white. It is believed that the period of illumination transmitted to the brain by the optic nerve affects the pituitary gland which produces hormones controlling both reproduction and molt.

Some years ago I became curious as to whether elevation could alter the coat color of varying hares. It was well known that while members of this species turned white in winter in the higher mountains and in the north, members of the same species living in lower coastal regions remained brown. I was fortunate to obtain three hares from a locality close to where I had studied pikas in the central Sierra Nevada of California at an elevation of 6,200 feet. This was in the Lake Tahoe basin where there is deep winter snow and the varying hares all assume a white winter coat. I kept these animals for some years in San Francisco, which is at sea level. Each autumn, at the same time, they molted from their brown summer coat to a white winter one which was maintained until the following spring. This seemed proof enough that altitude was not a factor and that the variable condition was under genetic control.

Another member of the weasel family that occasionally preys on pikas is the pine marten (*Martes americana*) in western North America. Pine martens are about the size of a small house cat but their bodies are more slender. Their fur is brown on the back and sides and often a deep orange yellow on the chest and underside of the neck. Martens, unlike their relatives the weasels living in high mountains, do not assume a white winter coat.

Martens are primarily dwellers of high coniferous forests, but in the mountains of western North America they often inhabit rocky slopes in summer where their principal food consists of deer mice, bushy-tailed wood rats, marmots, golden-mantled ground squirrels, and pikas. They do not seem to be in the rockslides in winter. At that season they restrict their activities to coniferous forests where they forage in the trees for red squirrels, flying squirrels, and even woodpeckers.

Pine martens are extremely agile and can move over rockslides with great ease. Their senses are very acute, and they have great endurance. In trees, they can move swiftly like a squirrel. In fact, the first time I saw a pine marten in the mountains I mistook it at first for a tree squirrel. Pine martens may be solitary or move in small packs, judging from their tracks in the snow in winter. They have fairly extensive territories and individuals have been known to travel as much as ten or fifteen miles in a single night. Much of their travel, however, is through the trees.

L. M. Lutton, who studied the response of pikas to predators, has commented on the marked difference in the reactions of pikas to different kinds of carnivores. A part of their defense to bear, lynx, or a large bird is to give an alarm call which is heeded by other members of the colony. They react the same way to the presence of a pine marten approaching a rockslide. Although this may call the marten's attention to the calling individual, it serves as a means of informing other pikas so that they may follow this carnivore's movements. Despite the fact that the marten can move over the rocks very rapidly, it is too large to penetrate the crevices into which the pikas retreat, and they move rapidly as the enemy approaches.

A quite different behavior is exhibited when a weasel is detected. At such times pikas are notably silent, not wanting to be seen by this small carnivore that can go wherever they can. When the weasel leaves the rockslide then calling begins.

While weasels are active both day and night, pine martens are principally nocturnal. Fortunately for the small animals on which it preys, but not for the pine marten, it is sought after for its fur. As a result of long persecution by trappers, these animals are not too common in many areas. Furthermore, they are extremely shy and stay away from areas inhabited by man.

There are other carnivorous mammals that may on occasion prey on pikas. One of these is the ubiquitous coyote (*Canis latrans*), a species that may be found from below sea level in Death Valley, California, to over 14,000 feet elevation in the high mountains of the West. Wherever there are small terrestrial mammals, there are likely to be coyotes. Rockslides are no exception and are periodically visited by these members of the dog family.

Hawks, eagles, and even, on occasions, owls may be important enemies of pikas in some localities. In the higher mountains of western North America, golden eagles, goshawks, and large hawks of the genus *Buteo* are all potential enemies and occur in areas where pikas are common. Broadbooks noted that "a hawk (*Buteo* sp.) flying over a rockslide excited five or six pikas into giving a number of alarm notes, and on another occasion a large hawk that flew down to the ground near camp caused a five-minute flurry of calling by both chipmunks and pikas."

Loukashkin lists the main enemies of the northern pika as the Siberian yellow mink (*Mustela siberica*) and the yellow ermine (*Mustela alpina*) which he says "freely penetrate into the pikas' burrows."

Ognev states that "The Daurian pika has many enemies. In winter it is hunted by snow owls, corsac foxes, and wolves. According to N. M. Przheval'skii, pikas suffer a lot from eagles and buzzards. This author writes: 'The ability of these birds of prey is amazing. I witnessed buzzards repeatedly swooping so rapidly on an ogotona that the animal did not have time to dash into its burrow.' We once saw the same done by an eagle who swooped on a pika sitting near the entrance of its burrow from a height of at least 30-40 sajenes." A sajene is 2.134 meters. Ognev also mentions that buzzards (*Circaetus ferox*) feed so extensively on pikas in the Gobi Desert that their wintering sites are mainly chosen in connection with the pika population.

Parasites

There is hardly a living thing that is not parasitized by some other organism, and pikas are no exception. Like their larger relatives, hares and rabbits, one of their principal ectoparasites are bot fly (*Cuteribra* sp.) larvae. The adult fly lays its eggs in the skin of the host, and the larva grows to full size before it emerges to pupate. A large lesion is produced under the skin as the larva grows. The upper hindquarters and the chest are common sites for these larvae, which are commonly called warbles. Haga reports that one out of twenty northern pikas (*Ochotona hyperborea yesoensis*) from Japan that were examined by him were infected with these larvae and in one instance thirty were found on a single animal.

Four species of fleas have been recorded from American pikas. Two of these, *Amphalius necopinus* and *Ctenophyllus terribilis*, occur on both *Ochotona collaris* and *O. princeps*. Both species are closely related to Siberian forms and may just be subspecies of the latter. Another flea, *Monopsyllus tolli*, is an Asiatic species that has been found on *Ochotona collaris* in Alaska. The fourth species, *Geusibia ashcrafti*, is known only from specimens of *Ochotona princeps* taken in California and Colorado. Its nearest relatives of the same genus are known from China.

Other common ectoparasites of pikas are trombiculid mites of the genus *Trombicula*. These commonly occur on the ears of their host. Ognev also describes a small parasitic tick which has been found on the ears of *Ochotona alpina*.

Pikas are infected with several species of nematode worms. The genus *Eugenuris* is found in *Ochotona collaris* and in Asian pikas, but not in *O. princeps* as far as known. Separate species of *Labiostomum* occur in pikas of Asia as well as in *Ochotona collaris* and *O.*

princeps. The nematode genus *Cephalurus* has separate species in pikas from Afghanistan, Alaska, and Colorado.

Pikas seem to do poorly in captivity unless they have sufficient room to carry on normal activities. When kept in the laboratory they show a high incidence of pneumonic symptoms and aspergillosis and are generally unsatisfactory as laboratory animals. O. Doyle Markham and F. W. Whicker, however, successfully captured and maintained "colonies" of these animals in two one-acre enclosures at Fort Collins, Colorado. They were taken in No. 1 Havahart traps that were placed near haystacks and dens. The traps were baited with dandelions, apples, sunflower seeds, and commercial rabbit food. Trapping success was greatest when pikas were busily engaged in building haypiles in late summer and autumn. No serious territorial combats occurred when captured pikas were released in one-acre pens in June, although chases did. But by July and August strong aggression was displayed when pikas were released in enclosures. In the more serious combats, opponents would stand on their hind legs and attempt to bite each other on the head and neck. Sometimes they would roll over together on the ground, each holding the other in its teeth. Cuts and bruises resulted from this and the defeated individual might be chased 100 feet from the disputed territory. It is questionable if such severe battles occur regularly in the wild.

Autumn

The Changing Season

As AUTUMN APPROACHES, the activities of most plants slow down. For all except a few late-blooming species, the flowering season is over and the seeds have matured. In the Sierra Nevada and Cascades as well as the Rocky Mountains in western North America, the aspens are assuming a golden hue. The green summer leaves that moved with the slightest breeze because their petiole, leaf stem, was flat instead of round, now dazzle the eye with their brilliance. They still quake with the wind as the scientific name *Populus tremuloides* would indicate, but with each gust a few fall to the ground. The creek dogwood is also changing color and assuming a delicate shade of pink, while the mountain maples are golden red.

The leaves of many other trees and shrubs, including willow, alder, mountain ash, and bitter cherry, are showing similar color changes. The pigments that produce the beautiful colors of autumn foliage were present all spring and summer but went unnoticed because they were obscured by the green chlorophyll which was so important for growth. The red, blue, and purple, as well as the yellow pigments, are contained in plant cells called chromoplasts. In autumn, the chlorophyll, which in the previous months was essential for photosynthesis and carbohydrate production, begins to break down. Gradually, with the disappearance of the green coloring matter, the other pigments become dominant until the leaves fall and the deciduous trees and shrubs are bare.

These same changes take place, although a few weeks earlier, farther north in North America as well as in Eurasia. In Alaska and parts of Canada the most obvious deciduous trees are the birches. Likewise, in northern Asia, from Siberia and Manchuria westward, the birches and aspens are also undergoing similar changes. These are all correlated with the changing daylength. The days gradually become shorter and the nights longer after the summer solstice in June, but the period of daylight as compared to darkness is very much greater for a long time yet. In mid-summer the sun is visible twenty-four hours a day in the north polar area. Before the autumnal equinox in September, however, the decrease in daylength becomes more and more noticeable in the Northern Hemisphere. The days also are cooler as the angle of the sun becomes greater and greater. The nights likewise are cooler, and the surface of the earth seems to be losing the warmth of summer. Occasional rainstorms occur and even when the sky is clear there is dew in the morning.

All these changes have a great effect upon living things, both plant and animal, in the North. It is not only apparent in the autumn coloration but also in other ways. Small annual plants, for the most part, have gone to seed and withered away. Many perennial shrubs have already produced their fruits or berries while others have just matured. The cones of pines, firs, and spruces are shedding their seeds one way or another. Some cones, like those of many pines, open their scales and fall to the ground. Others, such as firs, disintegrate on the branches that bear them and thereby release their seeds.

Other forms of plant life not so evident during most of the summer make their appearance. The rich litter of conifer needles and the leaves of other trees that have accumulated for years, forming a mat on the forest floor, seem to come alive. The lower temperatures and increased moisture have stimulated the growth of many kinds of fungi. From the tiny strands of mycelia that have lain hidden and dormant beneath the surface, there suddenly appears a whole assortment of weird and colorful structures which we commonly call mushrooms or toadstools, depending on whether or not they are edible. Some of the tiny mycenas are like fairy parasols and last for but a day or only a few hours. The inky caps and shaggy manes are much larger, but they too are very short-lived and, after maturing rapidly, break down into an inky mass by which they release their spores to possibly produce new fungus plants.

Many fungi are large and fleshy and provide food for a host of other organisms. Some kinds of flies have their life cycle geared to the fungus season. As soon as the fruiting bodies of these plants push up from the leaf mold and begin to expand, these insects lay their eggs in the soft structures on the underside of the cap. In some species these structures are gill-like, in others they may consist of tiny tubes joined together into a spongelike mass. In any event, the eggs hatch very rapidly once they are deposited. The maggots or larvae also grow very fast. This is necessary because the host, which is the fruiting body of the fungus, only lasts a few days, after which it either decomposes or dries up, depending on the weather as well as the composition of the fungus itself. By that time the larvae have matured and entered a pupal stage in the substratum where they will remain in a dormant condition until the same season the following year. At the proper time they will emerge as adult flies and start the process all over again.

During the fungi's short fruiting season, many animals partake of mushrooms in the forest, including snails and slugs. Among vertebrates we find that deer regularly eat many kinds of fungi, and red squirrels store them for future use. Food studies made on the habits of deer mice, so common over much of North America, show that small tuberous fungi growing beneath the surface of the forest litter are important in their diet.

As autumn approaches and the breeding season ends for birdlife, a physiological change begins. Territorial defense, song, nest building, and the rearing of young, at least once and sometimes twice, has required an enormous amount of energy. Now that this is over it is time to molt, a process which involves the loss of old feathers and the rapid growth of new to replace them. These amazing structures which maintain body temperature, provide protection, and make flight possible, are non-living once they are fully formed. Despite their delicate appearance they are remarkably durable. After many months of constant use, subject to oxidation, abrasion, and fading, they show wear and must be replaced.

Many birds have a partial change in plumage in the spring, especially the males, and a few have two complete molts a year. Ptarmigan are in the latter category. These grouse of the arctic and alpine heights of our western mountains are ground dwellers and live in an environment that is largely covered with snow for half of the year. In the high Cascades and Rocky Mountains the white-tailed ptarmigan inhabits the same rocky slopes as pikas. All during the summer their feathers are mostly brown. Although the white wings, tail, and belly are conspicuous when they fly, they blend beautifully into the drab background above timberline when on the ground. In autumn they molt and acquire a completely white plumage which makes them inconspicuous during the winter. Only their eyes and bill are black. In spring, when the snow is melting, this protectively colored winter plumage is again replaced by the brown.

Few other North American birds show this great contrast in

plumage coloration between summer and winter. All, however, have a complete molt at the end of the breeding season, usually in early fall. Early migrants molt before the year-round residents for various reasons. They need new, strong, flight feathers to sustain them during travel to their wintering grounds; some species that summer in the mountains winter far south in Mexico and Central America. Another reason for early molting in migrants concerns energy requirements. The production of a complete set of new feathers utilizes a great deal of bodily energy. So does the process of migration. It would overtax the body of most birds to molt and migrate at the same time. Consequently most migrant species molt first and then build up a surplus of body fat in early autumn to provide the necessary fuel to travel.

The young, hatched in spring and summer, must also molt. When first hatched they were naked or else had a natal down which was soon replaced by a juvenal plumage that had grown out by the time they were fledged. Many young birds in summer are distinguished by streaked or spotted feathers on the breast and side. In late summer or autumn, however, they molt into their first winter plumage which, for many, must last for the next twelve months.

Resident birds like jays or chickadees are not pressured to molt as early as migrants. Their lives are a bit more leisurely since they are already in their winter homes. Yet they too must replace their plumage in its entirety before the arrival of winter. Since their winter environment will be much more severe than that of most migrants, new feathers are essential for survival. These structures will provide a layer of still air which serves as insulation against the penetration of cold and also reduces the loss of body heat. On very cold days these birds fluff out their feathers to increase the thickness of the insulation just as we add more warm clothing to effect the same result. When it is warmer, the feathers are drawn closer to the body and the insulation is reduced.

Even before the leaves begin to turn there are other noticeable changes in the birdlife of the higher mountains. The white-crowned and Lincoln's sparrows, as well as the Wilson's warblers that nested in the willow and alder thickets bordering the streams in the mountain meadows, have gone. The silence now is broken only by the harsh calls of the Clark's nutcrackers flying down to lower levels each morning to feed. On slopes where mountain ash grows, its brilliant orange berries are now attracting small flocks of pine grosbeaks. The males, with their beautiful soft rose-colored heads and breasts, and the greenish gray females and immatures are mostly family groups. So quietly do they feed that one is hardly aware of their presence until their call notes attract attention. This is how I once began a study of their autumn habits. It was late September and I was observing pikas on a rockslide high above the western shore of Lake Tahoe in the central Sierra Nevada when I heard these calls from an ash thicket. Since these birds are rare and little was known of their habits, I returned the next day and found that they were feeding in the same place. For the next week or so pine grosbeaks replaced pikas as the object of research. It was a strenuous study because it entailed a climb of over 2,000 feet in elevation up a very steep mountain slope, through dense brush, and up treacherous rockslides to reach the site. The results were worth the effort and led to a publication on the autumn feeding behavior of that species.

In the alpine areas above timberline where rosy finches were nesting in late spring, even before some pika slides were freed of snow, these birds aggregate into sizable flocks. They do not move into the forests below nor will they. If winter forces them, they will descend to valley grasslands between mountain ranges or even to the desert, but they are not forest inhabitants. During the autumn, their foraging will be between loose pieces of granite and over slabs of rock where seeds as well as insects are sought. While seemingly rare and hard to find during the nesting season, they may be abundant locally in the fall. One may see pikas and rosy finches within a few feet of each other, each feeding in their own way.

Somewhat lower down the mountain slopes, other changes in the avian populations of the previous summer have taken place. A few of the yellow-rumped warblers, so common in the middle zone coniferous forests of western North America during the breeding season, remain. Most, however, have left by mid-September and will be found in the lowlands where insect food will still be available to them in the air, on the ground, and on the smaller branches of trees. They are most versatile feeders. Gone completely are the small flycatchers, the wood pewee, and the large olive-sided flycatcher whose loud call from a tree-top perch can be heard a quarter of a mile away during the summer. Gone also are the house wrens and the vireos that showed great preference for the now-yellowing aspens. Juncos have formed into flocks in preparation for their journey south or to lower levels.

Just as birds must replace their plumage by the autumn of the year, so must mammals acquire a new coat of hair or fur. Hair, like a feather once it is formed, is a non-living structure that is continually subject to wear and must be replaced at least annually. Hair in mammals serves many of the functions that feathers perform for birds. One of these is protection against enemies. The quills of a porcupine, which are really stout, sharp hairs, do this admirably. So also does the color of many small mammals. The pigment in the hairs of their coat is such that the animal blends in with its background, making it difficult for enemies to see it. This is true even among larger species. For example, the spotted coat of the fawn as it lies in the grass so disrupts its outline that its presence will go undetected by a passing carnivore that could easily outrun it. And, as already mentioned, other species have a white fur in winter and a brown fur in summer to adapt to the color change of their environment.

Thermoregulation, of course, is the greatest function performed by hair. Mammals, like birds, are warm-blooded vertebrates. Unlike reptiles that derive most of their body heat from the sun, mammals and birds produce their own by burning up fuel in their bodies. This, of course, requires a large intake of food. A large snake may eat once or twice a month, but a shrew in a mountain meadow must consume its own weight in food every twenty-four hours or starve and die of cold.

Heat conservation, therefore, is vital to mammals living in cold climates, and it is of particular importance to those species that are active all winter. A thick coat of hair or fur, then, acts like a bird's feathers in preventing the loss of body heat and the penetration of cold from the air.

Migration to a more favorable environment is but one of the ways that some mammals, like many birds, avoid the rigors of winter, while others stay and must make the necessary preparations. Many mammals that remain, like the pika, are going to be active all winter, but some will go into a state of torpidity that varies with different species. Since hibernation is a time when bodily activities are greatly reduced and food is not taken for months, there are certain things which must be done.

Some of the close associates of pikas in the mountain rockslides are among the greatest hibernators. These are the marmots and the ground squirrels. As autumn comes, the yellow-bellied marmot spends much of its time feeding and is in a physiological condition that results in a heavy deposition of fat on the body. Long before food becomes scarce and the first snows fall, these animals go deep into their burrows or dens where their body temperatures drop to about that of the environment. Their respiration rate, likewise, is greatly reduced. During their long winter sleep they slowly burn up the fat accumulated in autumn. This provides sufficient energy to sustain life in a state of suspended animation.

Golden-mantled ground squirrels behave in a somewhat similar manner although they may not hibernate quite as early as the marmots. During their winter torpidity their respiration rate may drop to as low as thirty times an hour as compared with sixty times a minute when awake and resting. In both animals there is a complete cessation of all body excretions until the following spring. Other important changes occur in the circulatory system. Studies on captive marmots show that in summer when at rest, a pulse of about ninety beats per minute is normal. When they are in hibernation it may drop to ten or twelve beats per minute. That of dormant ground squirrels may be less than six per minute. One might wonder why this great slowing down in the circulation of the blood doesn't cause clotting. To prevent this, the body shows a marked decrease in prothrombin production, the substance that causes clotting.

The Columbian ground squirrel, which often occurs in the same areas as golden-mantled ground squirrels and yellow-bellied marmots in southern Canada and northwestern United States, hibernates about eight months of the year. It too accumulates a large amount of fat in late summer and is ready for its winter sleep as soon as autumn arrives. Like many underground hibernators, this species builds its winter chamber in a side tunnel off the summer burrow system and lines it with dry vegetation. To reduce the penetration of external cold, the entrance to this chamber is plugged off.

The small, mountain-dwelling relative of the marmot and ground squirrel—the chipmunk—may be active all winter if the climate is temperate. Where there is considerable snow, some species store food and may even come out on nice days while others go into a completely torpid state.

Bears, both black and grizzly, go into a partial hibernation in winter. They select dens in the holes of trees or in caves where they stay in a reduced metabolic state. They do not eat and there is a complete cessation of excretion, but their body temperature remains close to normal even though the rate of respiration is much reduced. Unlike complete hibernators, they may easily be aroused.

Migration and hibernation are two ways in which animals prepare for winter. There are others that harvest much or all of their food and cache it away in the autumn for the winter season. Most of these are seed eaters. Seeds, such as those of pines and firs, are highly nutritious and store very well.

In September and October one cannot walk far in the coniferous mountain forests without encountering the kitchen middens of red squirrels. These are piles of cone scales where the squirrels have dismantled the cones for their nuts. They may be on the ground at the base of a tree, on a log, or even on a rock at the edge of a rockslide inhabited by pikas. Let the camper beware if he has his sleeping bag under a large fir in September. By sunrise, or shortly thereafter, the squirrels begin to cut the cones, and a mature fir cone falling fifty to a hundred feet can inflict a very severe injury to the face or head. There is security inside a tent but the thud of a hit is startling. While most mountain pines drop their cones whole when the seeds mature, this is not true of firs. The cones disintegrate on these trees and each scale falls separately until nothing is left but the upright axis to which they were attached. The squirrels, however, cut off their fir cones before this occurs. An individual red squirrel, after cutting a number of green fir cones, comes down the trunk to the ground, gathers them one at a time, and takes them to the midden site where, with sharp incisors, he cuts off the scales to free the seeds. After a sufficient number of seeds are collected in the cheek pouches inside the squirrel's mouth, it searches over the forest floor for a suitable place to bury them. This routine goes on for weeks and the size and number of the middens in the forest increases steadily.

Red squirrels also harvest fleshy fungi and store them in the crotches of trees for later use in winter.

The common tree squirrel of the forested parts of Europe and northern Asia, *Sciurus vulgaris*, has similar habits. According to Professor Ognev, it begins to feed on conifer nuts in July and by late summer starts on mushrooms. The following comments are from the translation of his work *Mammals of the U.S.S.R. and Adjacent Countries*: "In autumn its [*Sciurus vulgaris*] diet consists mainly of fresh mushrooms and pine nuts. During this period it begins to store mushrooms for the winter. Gol'tsmaier found the first dried mushrooms (*Boletus luteus*) in early August which apparently had been collected in late July." He then quotes Gol'tsmaier as follows: "The Teleut squirrel collects mushrooms with stems. It carefully carries one in its teeth to the nearest tree, where it pushes it into a fork of two branches or between the stems and a branch. The mushroom is arranged so that its pileus lies above two branches or hangs down from them. When it is dry it shrinks and surrounds the branch. It is so firmly fixed that neither wind nor shaking makes it fall. . . . Most mushrooms are stored on pine trees, as these are most numerous. A smaller number is found on birch, aspen, willow, and yellow acacia. . . . The squirrel chooses forks from thirty centimeters to four meters high for this. Mushrooms stored low down are later buried by snow. However, they are not lost and the squirrel digs them out from the snow."

The storage of mushrooms by tree squirrels is rather unique. It is probable that few if any other wild mammals have developed this habit. The autumn storage of seeds and nuts is by contrast a widespread occurrence, not only among spermophiles active in winter in the mountains, but also among many rodents in desert areas.

Few herbivores besides pikas store dry vegetation for winter use. One mammal that may possibly have this habit is the mountain beaver (*Aplodontia rufa*) of the Pacific slope of western North America. This animal is not to be confused with the true beaver

(*Castor canadensis*). The latter is an aquatic mammal and the largest native rodent in North America. The mountain beaver is a medium-sized, stocky rodent about twelve to fourteen inches long with a barely visible tail. It occurs in the Pacific northwest and from the central Sierra Nevada north to southern British Columbia. Mountain beavers often live in dense streamside thickets or in lush vegetation along seepages where they build a series of tunnels and exposed-surface runways. Frequently they divert water from streams or rivulets into their tunnel systems. This may be a means of increasing the kinds of vegetation on which they subsist—vegetation such as bracken fern, columbine, lilies, grasses, creek dogwood, alder, willow, and other moisture-loving plants.

In late summer and autumn, mountain beavers begin to build haypiles not unlike those of pikas. I have actually found the haypiles of the two species within less than a hundred yards of each other in the Sierra Nevada. These piles are stacks of fresh vegetation that are left for a few days to dry in the open. When the vegetation is dry it is taken into the burrow. The mountain beaver's haypile is usually located close to a tunnel entrance, and there has been considerable speculation as to whether this material is stored for winter food or whether it is nesting material. These animals are active all winter and construct extensive burrow systems beneath the snow in the higher mountains. These snow tunnels sometimes lead to deciduous trees whose bark is consumed at that season of the year.

The true beaver, while not closely related to the mountain beaver, also stores food for winter in cold regions. These animals have the habit of building dams of logs, branches, and mud across creeks and thereby forming so-called beaver ponds. This insures a permanent source of water and increases the available shore line for the growth of willow, aspen, and other trees requiring considerable moisture. Such ponds also provide sites for beaver houses whose entrances are under water. In autumn, before the surface of these ponds freezes, beavers cut numerous trees nearby and drag them to the pond where they are submerged. When winter comes, the bark, branches, and twigs sealed under the ice provide the beavers with food in complete safety from predators.

Most of the birds that remain in mountainous regions where there is extensive snowfall and low temperatures in winter are rather specialized insect eaters. Nuthatches, chickadees, creepers, and various kinds of non-migratory woodpeckers obtain adult or larval insects mostly from the bark of trees; nature stores their winter food for them. Jays may store food in bark or branch crevices and under litter on the ground. It is questionable whether such storage is anything more than temporary.

Blue grouse, whose deep ventriloquial hoot is heard on many mountain slopes in the spring even though the calling males are seldom seen, winters in a somewhat different manner. In autumn, family groups, adults and the young of the year now nearly of full size, begin to ascend the mountains in a sort of reverse migration. By the time the winter storms come they are in dense clumps of trees, particularly firs, where they will remain until spring. The conifer buds provide them with sufficient food during this period.

Another member of the crow and jay family that lives in the same general environment as the pika in much of its range in North America and does store winter food is Clark's nutcracker. These birds of the high mountains are largely dependent in winter on the seeds of various pines and firs they have stored in autumn. The white-bark pine, a timberline species, is one of their important food sources. In years when there is a low production of cones and, consequently, seeds, there may be irruptions of nutcrackers and mass movements of these birds to the lowlands where they do not normally occur.

The harvesting of vegetation for the winter
food supply starts in mid-summer and
continues through autumn until
stopped by snow.
(*Photograph by Douglas B. Herr*)

The Haypile

While autumn is a time when plants and animals of the Northern Hemisphere are preparing for the arrival of winter, it is also a time of change in the behavioral activities of the pika. This is an animal that is, in a sense, colonial, yet it is also aggressive toward its neighbor. Pikas live adjacent to one another, not isolated on individual rockslides. In spring this aggression is at a low, there is some tolerance of other individuals and brief pairing of males and females for reproductive purposes. As summer arrives aggression increases and tolerance decreases, especially after the young are independent. This behavioral pattern results in the delineation of individual territories and their defense by the owner. With the arrival of autumn, aggressive behavior by individual animals reaches its peak and numerous encounters occur. An invader, when detected, is given chase, although this usually stops at the edge of the territory. While the sex or age of the invader makes no difference in the defense, there are differences in the degree of social dominance. Larger and more aggressive individuals tend to have the best territories, rockslide areas immediately adjacent to feeding grounds. This development of a strong territorial behavior after the reproductive season is rather unique among warm-blooded vertebrates and serves a very different purpose from the breeding territories of many other kinds of animals.

From spring until the latter part of summer, pikas feed daily on the various edible plants available to them adjacent to the rockslides. As aggressive behavior increases in summer, harvesting also increases, and more and more haypiles are formed. By the time autumn arrives, pikas everywhere in western North America are devoting a major part of their active time to gathering and drying stacks of vegetation for winter use and defending them against other individuals. Throughout Eurasia, from the Urals to Manchuria, most

North American pikas stack their hay under
rocks, on rocks, and in crevices between rocks.
(*Photograph by Douglas B. Herr*)

kinds of pikas are exhibiting a somewhat similar pattern of behavior.
There are, though, a few exceptions.

With increased aggression and strong territorial defense as well
as the urge to accumulate haypiles, there is a gradual decrease in
caution. This has been noted by a number of observers. Pikas are
very wary in spring when the snow has melted, but as the summer
comes they become bolder. This seems to be related to activity. David
P. Barash's studies on pikas in Glacier National Park, Montana,
showed that haying and feeding trips were statistically indistinguish-
able in June, but in July and August there was a significant increase
in the frequency of haying trips while the frequency of those concerned with feeding did not change. It was also noted that young
just out of the nest began both haying and feeding trips and, like
the adults, they devoted more time to haying than feeding before
summer ended.

Most of the feeding areas used are in the open, although some
are partly protected by scattered shrubs. When going out to feed, a
pika first carefully watches its surroundings from the protection of
the rockslide. It then moves rapidly to the feeding site, sometimes
pausing briefly once or twice en route. When feeding, an adult pika
generally cuts the vegetation close to the ground and, after a brief
glance around, consumes it on the spot. By way of contrast, juveniles
usually consume the vegetation in place, starting at the top and
working toward the base of the plant. Between June 1 and August
12, Barash timed forty-seven feeding trips and found them to average
2.2 minutes as contrasted with an average of 1.0 minutes for thirty-
six haying trips. When vegetation is gathered for the haypile it is
usually pulled up near the roots; as soon as a mouthful is gathered,
it is brought back to the haypile. The plants are carried crosswise
in the mouth in the process. In places where the rockslides used by
pikas are surrounded by brush instead of open spaces grown with
small herbs, pikas will feed on these shrubs and also use them in

Vegetation for the haypile is cut near the base or pulled up from the ground. It is carried crossways and held near the base of the cut stems by the teeth. The paws are not used to hold the food.

(*Photograph by Douglas B. Herr*)

their winter store piles. This usually requires them to stand on their hind legs to cut off twigs. I have frequently observed this in regions where bitter cherry, huckleberry oak, and snowbush are abundant. On one occasion I watched a pika climb to the top of a rock that was next to a bush and stand on its hind legs to reach a twig several feet above the ground.

Feeding and hay gathering are individual activities among American pikas. Each animal has its own feeding area and guards its own haypiles. These piles are variously situated. Sometimes they are accumulated under rocks where little sun reaches them, but more often they are in the open where the hay can be sun-cured. Occasionally the hay is piled up against old logs on the edge of rockslides. Each haypile is added to daily until it is about two feet high and about the same in diameter.

Some of the haypiles are left out all winter but others may be taken apart, with the dried plants taken in under the cover of rocks. There is, however, some question about this. Markham and Whicker found that captive pikas made no attempt to move vegetation from the original haystacks. They concluded, as have others, that in the natural habitat there is no attempt to dry or move collected vegetation, nor do they gather it under shelter when storms approach. Early storms and strong winds sometimes blow the tops off the taller stacks. The stacks may be conical but more often large stacks are shaped like a farmer's haystack with nearly vertical sides. The animal always adds to the top and in so doing may stand on its hind legs. The vegetation is arranged with the mouth; the front feet are never involved in this activity.

Some pikas may construct only one haypile at a time, others build two or more simultaneously, alternating their activities between the piles. The weather has a definite effect on haying activities. During clear, sunny days, activity peaks are reached in the morning and again in mid-afternoon with a definite lull in the middle of the day.

An old haypile from the previous year.

Inclement weather greatly reduces above-ground activity and heavy rain may cause the animals to stay in entirely.

The composition of the haypile is dependent on the species of food plants present. Pikas generally are not very selective and will eat a great variety of available species. In western Montana, haypiles have been seen containing wild raspberry (*Rubus strigosus*), mountain cranberry (*Vaccinium vitis-idaea* var. *minus*), Oregon grape (*Berberis repens*), twinflower (*Linnaea borealis*), lungwort (*Mertensia paniculata*), and chokecherry (*Prunus virginiana* var. *demissa*). The raspberry was used in greater quantity than the other species.

Broadbook has recorded at least twenty-three species of plants stored in some abundance in the northern Cascades of Washington. Species most preferred were lupine (*Lupinus sulphureus*), vetch (*Lathyrus lanszwertii*), a composite (*Luina stricta*), and dwarf huckleberry (*Vaccinium scoparium*). *Luina* and *Lathyrus* were found in sixteen haypiles, *Lupinus* in eleven, and *Vaccinium* in seven. Some other plants found in a number of the haypiles were manzanita (*Arctostaphylos* sp.), aspen (*Populus tremuloides*), *Arnica* sp., buckwheats (both *Eriogonum compositum* and *E. umbellatum*), yarrow (*Achillea millefolium*), *Phacelia heterophylla*, ocean-spray (*Holodiscus discolor*), snowberry (*Symphoricarpos albus*), *Balsamorhiza careyana*, elderberry (*Sambucus* sp.), scarlet gilia (*Ipomopsis aggregata*), sagebrush (*Artemisia tridentata*), grasses, sedge, lichen, and juniper (*Juniperus* sp.) twigs. Broadbook also reported a haypile composed of fresh cut twigs from a Douglas fir (*Pseudotsuga menziesii*) that was forty feet away. One of the limbs of the tree touched the ground, and the pika was seen climbing it to cut off twigs. On two occasions the animal fell to the ground as a result of its arboreal ventures. Once it dropped two feet and again about one foot.

The use of coniferous twigs for food or haypiles for winter is not

Remains of an old haypile between
some large rocks.

In early September the haypiles of the Daurian
pikas in the Altai Mountains of Outer
Mongolia were composed of two species of
Artemisia. The cut plants were laid on the
pile with the bases of the stems uppermost.

unusual but is dependent upon the ability of the animal to reach them. I have seen pikas in the Sierra Nevada carrying fresh red fir twigs where the low branches were available to them. In one of my study areas near Lake Tahoe, haypiles in late August were composed principally of bitter cherry (*Prunus emarginata*), huckleberry oak (*Quercus vaccinifolia*), snowbush (*Ceanothus cordulatus*), and bracken (*Pteridium aquilinum*). One haypile was in a rock crevice under a large boulder and was estimated to contain about one cubic yard of vegetation.

Haypiles seem to be stored in the same places year after year. Examination of new piles of vegetation shows the presence of old material from previous years at the base. Mention has previously been made of coprophagy, the habit of eating fecal pellets, in pikas. It is not uncommon to find the pellets of marmots in haypiles, and pikas have been seen eating these pellets as well as storing them for winter.

Broadbook's studies on the ecology of the American pika included data on the rate of growth of their haypiles. The average daily increase in the height of seven stacks in mid-August was .82 inches, which was nearly twice the rate of growth observed the previous month. One animal built a haypile twenty-two inches high in eighteen days ending August 13. One of the largest unsupported haypiles that Broadbook observed was twenty-four inches high and thirty-two inches wide at the base.

Haga made a study of the Japanese subspecies of the northern pika (*Ochotona hyperborea yesoensis*) to determine whether or not it could be domesticated as a laboratory animal. Special attention was given to the food plants utilized and various activities associated with food procuring and storage. As with most pikas, the plants eaten depended largely on the habitat and species available. Haga recorded twenty-eight species eaten or stored. These ranged from club mosses, ferns, and herbaceous plants to the leaves and twigs of deciduous trees such as birch, alder, maple, and linden. True hay-stack construction for winter use began in October and continued for one or two months until the snow came. The usual size of a com-pleted stack was about one meter (thirty-nine inches) in diameter and sixty centimeters (twenty-four inches) in height. An analysis of the composition of one unfinished stack in a spruce-fir forest (*Ochotona hyperborea* is a forest dweller) weighed 3.5 kilograms (approximately 8 pounds) on November 22 and contained 2 kilo-grams of wood fern, 600 grams of male fern, 420 grams of Alle-gheny spruce, 20 grams of bunch berry, 50 grams of small branches, and 300 grams of unidentifiable material. In this particular species it is believed that pairs often cooperate in the construction of hay-piles, unlike American pikas. Haga also observed that pikas often harvest vegetation which is stored in small piles in crevices in rocks. These, however, are not for winter use but are seemingly consumed within a few days. Apparently this species prefers partly dried vege-tation. This habit was observed even in summer when fresh green plants were most abundant. In captivity, this species consumed only thirty percent of its food during daylight hours.

In the lower parts of the south end of the Altai Mountains in Outer Mongolia in September 1976, I found the *Ochotona daurica* harvesting, almost exclusively, *Artemisia* of two species. Through the courtesy of Dr. Elizabeth McClintock, Curator of Botany at the California Academy of Sciences, one of these was identified as *Ar-temisia azerbajdzhan*. Because of the complexity of this plant genus in north central Asia, the identity of the second species has not yet been determined. Both species of plants were herblike in stature, equally common, and grew to a height of twelve to eighteen inches. Haypiles were usually located outside of burrow entrances or along well-defined trails within a few feet of a burrow entrance. The bur-row entrances were from three to five inches in diameter and the haypiles were located to either side of the entrance. It was not un-

Daurian pikas were so numerous in parts of
Outer Mongolia's Altai Mountains that they
even constructed haypiles under
man-made structures.

common to find a stack next to a burrow opening and another three or four feet away along the trail leading to the entrance. The vegetation in the haypiles was cut at the base of the plants; most of the twigs were in ten to twelve inch segments. The largest haypile that I observed was twenty-four inches in diameter and twelve inches in height.

The haypiles as well as the trails of *Ochotona daurica* were very conspicuous in the landscape and could be seen for a considerable distance. All of the plant material found in the stacks in early September was freshly cut. One haypile, interestingly, was found underneath the edge of a bench in a picnic area.

Others have observed the autumn behavior of the Daurian pika. Loukashkin writes of this species in Manchuria: "At the end of August these animals prepare their hay stocks for the wintertime. They cut off the grass stems at the root and bring them to selected places on the open ground surface, piling the grass in small cone-like heaps, arranging it so that the tops are below and cut ends above." I noted this same arrangement used for pieces of *Artemisia* in Mongolia, with the basal stems directed up and the heads down (see photo on page 114).

Loukashkin continues: "Such a haycock after drying weighs from two to five pounds. When drying their grass the pikas turn their haycocks over several times until they become well prepared hay. Many hundreds and sometimes even thousands of such minute cones can be seen in September, covering an area of two to three square kilometers occupied by the colony.

"The [Daurian] pika does not show preference for any particular kind of plants; it feeds on any kinds that occur. Various species of *Artemisia* constitute a considerable percentage in their stocks." The latter statement agrees with my own observations on the haypiles of this species.

Professor Ognev states that: "The Daurian pika prepares small

Two Daurian pika haypiles close together
along a trail coming from a burrow.

Some Daurian pika haypiles are placed right
next to the burrow entrance.

'haystacks' for winter in front of the entrance of the burrow. The hay serves both as bedding and as food in winter. The efforts of the rodents are often wasted as this hay is eaten by cattle. In this case the rodent has to live throughout the winter on dry grass which it finds under the snow." He lists the following plants which are eaten by these pikas according to their decreasing frequency: *Medicago ruthenica, Artemisia dracunculus, Potentilla tanacetifolia, Artemisia siversiana, Potentilla siberica,* and *Medicago falcata. Medicago* is a clover and *Potentilla* is a widespread northern genus belonging to the rose family. Ognev, quoting from the work of Formozov, says: "When the tips of the iris leaves have hardly begun yellowing in autumn, the pikas begin cutting them and piling them in large heaps near the burrows. The leaves are arranged in a star pattern and are moved from time to time. However, this does not prevent decay of some leaves deep in the heap. In addition to iris, the haystacks contain some grasses and artemisia. The stacks were about 50 cm wide and 35-40 cm high. Along the Dzabhan Gol, pikas, the burrows of which were on low land under willow roots, arranged their haystacks near stones, trees and on stumps."

Ognev also mentions that N. M. Przheval'skii found grasses, artemisia, composites, twigs of the peashrub, and other legumes in the haystacks. He also reports that G. I. Radde "says that pikas cover their haystacks with branches of peashrub or *Chenopodium* to prevent scattering by the wind."

Ognev provides a very good summary of the hay-storing habits of the alpine or Altai pika (*Ochotona alpina*). This is a species that inhabits screes and has its burrows between the stones. Food is stored in haypiles near the burrows or else under rocks. It may also be hoarded underground deep in the burrow system. Ognev quotes from Kuznetsov as follows: "In August when I collected material on the snow-covered Narym Mountains, I observed that the pikas were busy preparing hay for the winter. In the morning they could be observed scurrying among the stones of the scree carrying grasses to their nests. I found large stores of dried hay between the stones, solidly rammed into cracks. These hoards consisted of many different plants, but cereals were not represented in them at all."

Ognev continues to quote from other authors regarding the food-gathering habits of this species as follows: "The pika moves slowly, its movements like those of a calmly feeding rabbit. It examines the ground, paying particular attention to the yellow birch leaves which cover it. A suitable leaf is taken at the edge and borne to the burrow. The pika repeats this several times, and discards dozens of unsuitable leaves. When it becomes tired and hungry it chooses a leaf, calmly sits down and eats rapidly, moving its muzzle like a rabbit.

"Food-hoarding pikas do not only drag leaves into the burrow. They also store leaves on the ground, apparently using leaves driven by the wind under fallen trees."

The alpine pika in the Teletskoe Lake region on the Altai has been found to store the following plants in its haypile: *Rubus idaeus*, *Rosa acicularis*, *Athyrium filix-femina*, *Pteridium aquilinum*, *Saxifraga crassifolia*, *Lycopodium annotinum*, *Vaccinium vitis-idaea*, *Betula verrucosa*, *Sphagnum archangelica descerrens*, *Cystopteris fragilis*, *Carex* sp. It is evident from this list that this high mountain species has to eat ferns, mosses, club mosses, and birch leaves as well as shrubs and herbs because of the limited availability of the latter at this season at high elevations.

The storing habits of the Mongolian or Price's pika (*Ochotona pricei*), a species of scattered rocky outcrops on the desert, is best described by Ognev as follows: "Heaps of grass spread to dry may be found on densely populated rocks during the day. Large stores of hay fill large hollows in the rocks, or cavities under stones. The hay consisted of the following plants: 1) store in a niche among rocks on 30 Jul. 1926 in the lower reaches of river Tuin-Gol (♀84) —

Artemisia pectinata, Euratia coratoides, Carex stenophylla, Tanace-tum achillaeoides; 2) store under stones on 1 Sept. 1946 between rivers Baydarag Gol and Dzabhan Gol—*Tanacetum achillaeoides, Carex stenophylla, Artemisia* sp.; in a third case, grasses and *Aster altaicus* were found in addition to the above plants.

"When foraging, the pika is very cautious, hurrying to the rocks at the first alarm. However, after it reaches its refuge, it does not hide long in its burrow, but appears again outside after a short time. The traces in the sand indicate that *O. pricei* does not go farther than a few tens of meters from its burrows. It is fond of rocks, and moves rapidly over steep surfaces, and has a peculiar way of folding its rather large and broad ears. These habits make it easy to distinguish from the Daurian pika."

Very little seems to be known about the food storage habits of the northern pika (*Ochotona hyperborea*) throughout its range outside of Japan. This is a talus-inhabiting species that lives in crevices between stones, in cliff cavities, and in burrows under boulders. The best account is provided by Loukashkin who states: "The Manchurian pikas do not put their hay in the form of a conical heap. Instead of this they hide the hay in conveniently situated holes in trees and in the rotted out cavities of stumps, or sometimes under wind-felled tree trunks, and in cavities among rocks. Its hay stocks are piled in formless masses that may reach a weight of 15–40 pounds. All the hay stocks that I saw were located in safely hidden places."

The Japanese race of the northern pika (*Ochotona hyperborea yesoensis*) was studied by Kawamichi and in his article "Hay territory and dominance rank of pikas," he points out the difference in social structure between this species and *O. princeps* of North America. In the Japanese pika there is single mate pairing and mutual food collecting. As a result, there is a complete absence of territorial defense between members of a pair. Kawamichi also notes the correlation between haypiling and vocalization. In the Japanese pika, like the North American species, calling and the accumulation of haypiles are highly developed. By way of contrast, two Asian species, *Ochotona macrotis* and *O. royalei*, have weakly developed voices and essentially no haypiles. These two species engage in winter foraging.

Autumn terminates earlier in northern Asia than in the mountains of western North America. When it does, irrespective of locality, it represents the end of many strenuous, busy weeks and months of activity. When snow covers the vegetation the piling of hay becomes essentially impossible for these little animals, and activities must largely be confined beneath the surface.

Winter

WINTER IN THE HIGHER MOUNTAINS is a time of dormancy for the plant kingdom. The alders, birches, aspens, and willow stand leafless. The conifers have their needles, all except the larch, but growth is at a standstill. While the ground may be deep with snow, water is in a frozen state and not available to any extent for growth. The metabolic activity of these trees in late winter does produce some heat and the snow begins to melt around their trunks. The evergreen shrubs, like the conifers, remain quiescent even though they retain their leaves all winter. The flower buds of some, like the manzanita, are encased in snow waiting only for spring to release them.

Within the bark of the trees many insects are in dormancy. Some will spend the winter in a larval condition preparing for their emergence as adults when the days become longer and warmer. While well hidden in crevices or holes in the bark, many of them will fall victim to chickadees, nuthatches, and woodpeckers, whose sharp eyes and probing bills will seek them out for food.

Certain kinds of chipmunks will sleep throughout this period while others, differently adapted, will wake up occasionally and partake of food which they have stored close to their nest, underground, or deep within a snag. So too will the red squirrels, who had industriously stored myriads of seeds in the autumn and, while preparing this winter food, created numerous middens in the forest. On sunny days, even in mid-winter, they may come out and forage over the branches, giving an occasional call. Their relatives, the flying squirrels, are active every night except when the weather is too severe. Unlike most of the other members of the squirrel family in the northern part of the Northern Hemisphere, they do not engage in any kind of hibernation.

Winter is the season when porcupines den up in the mountains. Sometimes a dozen individuals will be aggregated deep in the protective cover of a great pile of boulders. There may also be a woodrat occupying the same rock pile. Woodrats are solitary animals and are active all winter. At night they come out to forage and search for twigs which are added to their houses in the rocks.

On a morning after a fresh fall of snow, the white surface on the forest floor will show the tracks of many animals that have been active during the night. Small prints of deer mice extend from log to log. Larger tracks made by varying hares indicate where these beautiful lagomorphs have been under the cover of darkness. They now have a pure white coat which makes them difficult for enemies to detect against the background of snow. Food is hard to find for meat eaters at this time of year, so these hares must depend upon their protective coloration and their ability to bound over the snow with broad, heavily haired hind feet if a hungry enemy approaches. Their greatest danger comes from coyotes which are active all winter in the mountains. They are also sought after by great gray owls, goshawks, eagles, and the ever-searching pine marten.

The tracks of pine martens in the snow tell a great deal about these wary members of the weasel family. Many times they appear to be solitary, but on occasions they travel in packs, or at least a number of individuals use the same trail during the night. Their hunting route may take them as much as ten to fifteen miles in a twenty-four-hour period. Much of the course is usually through forest where they may travel a considerable distance through the trees without coming to the ground. The hunting trails may lead to rockslides; whether or not they try to ferret out the inhabitants below we do not know. They are persistent hunters, however, and concentrate intently on their prey. One November afternoon, while I was standing quietly on a high ridge at about 8,500 feet elevation in the Sonora Pass region of the Sierra Nevada, I watched a marten following a red squirrel through the trees. It was extremely nimble and so squirrellike itself that at first I thought I was watching two squirrels. Neither animal saw me even though they passed within ten yards. This also proves that martens hunt by day as well as by night in winter. Despite their strength, pine martens are small enough to be captured occasionally by golden eagles, horned owls, and great gray owls.

The largest and most powerful member of the weasel family is the wolverine, which inhabits the boreal forests of northern North America and Eurasia. The literature is filled with stories of its audacity and strength. The name glutton has been applied to these animals by trappers who have had them rob the catches from their trap lines. Most wolverines in the West live near timberline where they search for any animal they can catch for food. Though they are no longer abundant, they must be reckoned with as a serious enemy, especially in winter. Even the porcupine is not immune to its attack.

Reproduction is at its lowest ebb in winter, yet this is the time when black bear cubs are born. Although the mother is in a semi-torpid condition during much of this season, her body temperature remains high, and she is easily awakened. The two or three young in the litter are very small at birth, weighing between one-half and three-quarters of a pound. While with the mother in the winter den, they nurse and grow. By the following spring they will be large enough to venture outside for short periods of play in the sunlight and by early summer accompany their mother in search of roots, grass, grubs, and various other food items.

Beneath the mantle of snow that covers not only the rockslides and forest floor but the meadows, there is other activity. Pocket gophers are probably more active in winter than in summer. In winter they extend their burrow systems from beneath the surface of the ground up into the snow. This enables them to invade a new habitat for food that is not safely available to them during the rest of the year. Under the protective cover of the snow, they may move above ground to shrubs which can provide food. They also secure bark from small deciduous trees. There still are bulbs and roots underground, but the extra supplement above helps compensate for the greater energy requirements that a warm-blooded vertebrate has in winter if it does not hibernate.

Another subterranean dweller, often associated with pocket gophers in the same meadows and semi-open forest land in some mountainous areas in western United States, is the broad-footed mole. These animals, however, avoid rocky areas because their lives are spent beneath the surface of the ground through which they burrow. Unlike pocket gophers, the presence of snow does not entice them to the surface. They are strictly non-vegetarians, living on earthworms and other small invertebrates in the soil.

One can follow the winter activities of mammals like the pocket gopher whose earth cores pushed out from underground tunnels into snow tunnels remain after the snow has melted. These sometimes lead to trees whose bark has been removed, telling more about their habits. More difficult to follow are the winter movements of moles. However, we find that their winter burrows are much like those of other seasons of the year, although subsurface foraging is not likely in winter since earthworms go deeper down so as not to freeze.

Active and competing in part with pocket gophers are the voles or meadow mice. These small, blunt-nosed rodents occur in grassland both in North America and Eurasia. In the Rocky Mountains, as well as the Sierra-Cascade ranges, these animals are active all winter beneath the snow. Some, like the lemming vole (*Phenacomys intermedius*), probably contact pikas many times in winter as well as summer. This species lives in heather patches along the margins of alpine meadows, frequently next to rockslides. It is possible that there is competition between these voles and some pika colonies for winter food. In other lower montane meadows, voles and pocket gophers also compete for winter food beneath the snow.

One can only guess what goes on under the snow in a rockslide inhabited by pikas. It seems likely that there still is territorial defense of haypiles which are vital for survival. Studies by Markham and Whicker on *Ochotona princeps* in captivity in Colorado in winter have shown that pikas construct tunnels under the snow. Within five days after a snowfall of fifteen to thirty centimeters, individuals had tunnels under the surface between every rock pile and every cage. This same type of behavior has been noted in this species in the wild in western North America. Haga found that the Japanese pikas (*Ochotona hyperborea yesoensis*) were active in winter on the top of the snow until it reached a depth of twenty to thirty centimeters, after which they constructed tunnels under the snow.

The marvelous adapation of these mammals, whereby they stockpile hay for winter, has been taken advantage of by other herbivores,

Winter snow seals the pika colonies from the
outer world for many months.

(*Photograph by James Moffitt*)

even larger ones. Loukashkin, writing about the northern pika in Manchuria, makes the following comment: "All the hay stocks that I saw were located in safely hidden places. This precaution enables the pikas to save their food from the forest robbers, among which are the Ussurian moose (*Alces alces bedfordi*), Siberian roe-deer (*Capreolus capreolus pygarus*) and varying hare (*Lepus timidus transbaicalicus*)." Loukashkin also comments on the problems to which the Daurian pika (*Ochotona daurica*) is subject: "Mongolian herders, knowing this peculiarity [haystacking] of the [Daurian] pikas, utilize their hay stocks in winter, when hardened deep snow covers the steppe, and grazing for the cattle and sheep becomes very difficult. The Mongolians drive their herds to localities where there are pika colonies and the hungry animals feed upon the pika stocks."

Dr. Roy Chapman Andrews made mention of the use by Mongolian herdsmen of the haypiles of pikas in the Gobi Desert. He reported that in times of dire need in winter, Mongolian herdsmen brought their herds, including Bactrian camels, to pika colonies where they could feed on the stores of these little animals. The Daurian pika is a prolific storer of vegetation and most all of its haypiles are on flat ground in the open. Even in early autumn, before the snow began to fall, I observed herds of yaks in the south end of the Altai Mountains feeding in areas where pika haypiles abounded. Food was still abundant at that time but it was easy to visualize a time later on in winter when only the haypiles would stick up above the snow and provide tempting morsels for large, hungry herbivores.

No doubt pikas of many species suffer severely from robbery of their winter stores. In North America there is little likelihood of large animals stealing from pika haypiles because of the type of habitat. Rock piles and talus covered with snow are not suitable for most large herbivores except mountain goats and bighorn sheep.

In Asia, however, those species that live in flat areas away from rocks are likely to have their stores preyed upon by most large herbivores, wild and domestic.

Small robbers may play a much more significant role in reducing the winter stockpiles of pikas than the larger ones, although we can only speculate on this. White-footed mice, woodrats, and other small vegetarians living in the talus with pikas probably take items suitable to their diet if they are available in pika haypiles.

One suspects that pikas must secure food other than that stored in autumn before the winter ends. Tunnels in the snow make it possible for them to extend their foraging activities in relative safety to areas adjacent to their rockslides. While succulent herbs are not available in winter, the leaves and bark of many shrubs are. These will provide nutrients to supplement stored foods or even replace them if the latter are somehow stolen or destroyed.

Winter certainly is the most critical season for these animals. They spend months under a blanket of snow where the temperature is probably around 32° F. Since they do not accumulate fat under the skin in the fall, they are dependent entirely on their fur for insulation and the winter food they have stored or can otherwise secure for energy. Their haypile caches are enormous however. Broadbooks found one pile containing, in mid-August, 10,860 cubic inches of well-packed, cured plants, as well as many marmot scats. He estimated that such a pile might be increased by one-half before the winter snow came.

Vocalization goes on in winter. Calling can be heard deep beneath the snow if one travels over an inhabited pika rockslide. Apparently pikas hear footsteps through many feet of covering. One wonders what function these call notes serve and if the sounds travel through the snow-covered talus from one animal's territory to that of another.

There are many mysteries about the winter behavior of these animals that have not yet been solved. One wishes that it were possible to delve into this snow-covered environment and remain unseen for just a while to find out how life goes on in an environment that is sealed off from the outer world for so many months. This part of the pika's world still remains unknown to those of us who seek to learn about its way of life.

Classification and Distribution

THERE IS SOME lack of uniform agreement on the classification of the various pikas of the world. The specific arrangement that follows is based upon the generally accepted classification given by Hall and Kelson for our North American species and Ellerman and Morrison-Scott for the Asiatic species. The latter do not entirely agree with Ognev's arrangement for some species found in the U.S.S.R. In the following list, fourteen living species of pikas are recognized. Two of these occur in North America, eleven are strictly Asiatic, and one occurs in both southeastern Europe and in Asia. No attempt has been made to list the many different subspecies that have been described.

Collared pika (*Ochotona collaris*)

Range: Central and southern Alaska, Yukon, and northern British Columbia.

Southern pika (*Ochotona princeps*)

Range: Rocky Mountains from central British Columbia and Alberta south to New Mexico; Cascades from southern British Columbia to northern California; the Sierra Nevada; isolated ranges in the Great Basin region.

Steppe or small pika (*Ochotona pusilla*)

Range: Southern Urals and Upper Volga east through Kazakhstan; occurring possibly in Kashmir, Yunnan, northern Assam, and northern Burma; within historic times this species had a more extensive range in southeastern Europe.

Moupin pika (*Ochotona thibetana*)

Range: Sikkim, northeastern India; Yunnan, Szechuan, Shensi, Shanzi, Kansu, and Hupeh provinces, China.

Royle's pika (*Ochotona royalei*)

Range: Nepal, Punjab, and Kashmir; Tibet; Szechuan and Yunnan provinces in western China; northern Burma.

Big-eared pika (*Ochotona macrotis*)

Range: Central Asia in the Pamir and Tienshan ranges, Kashmir, the Karokorum Mountains, northern Nepal, and southern Sinkiang Province, China.

Daurian pika (*Ochotona daurica*)

Range: From central Iran east to Tibet, Kansu, China, Mongolia, and the Altai region of Siberia.

Afghan pika (*Ochotona rufescens*)

Range: Parts of Uzbeckistan, Afghanistan, Iran, and Baluchistan.

Koslow's pika (*Ochotona koslowi*)

Range: Known only from northern Tibet.

Alpine or Altai pika (*Ochotona alpina*)

Range: Altai and Sayan mountains, Transbaikalian Mountains, Mongolia, and northern Kansu, China.

Northern pika (*Ochotona hyperborea*)

Range: Northern Urals in eastern Russia; Siberia from the Yenesei River east to Kamtchatka and Sakalin, north to the Arctic Ocean, and south to Mongolia, Manchuria, and Japan.

Pallas' pika (*Ochotona pallasi*)

Range: Kazakhstan and the Russian Altai; Mongolia; east end of the Tien Shan Range, Sinkiang Province, China. Ognev refers to this species as Price's pika (*Ochotona pricei*).

Red pika (*Ochotona rutila*)

Range: Eastern Uzbeckistan in the Pamir, Hissar-Alai, and Tien Shan ranges; Tibet; Kansu and Szechuan provinces, China.

Ladak pika (*Ochotona ladacensis*)

Range: Known from Kashmir; Tibet; Sinkiang Province, China.

Bibliography

Allen, Glover M. 1938. *The Mammals of China and Mongolia.* 2 vols. New York: American Museum of Natural History.

Andrews, Roy Chapman. 1932. "The new conquest of central Asia." *Natural History of Central Asia*, vol. 1. New York: American Museum of Natural History.

Barash, David P. 1973. "Territorial and foraging behavior of pika (*Ochotona princeps*) in Montana." *American Midland Naturalist* 89:202–207.

Broadbooks, Harold E. 1965. "Ecology and distribution of the pikas of Washington and Alaska." *American Midland Naturalist* 73:299–335.

Bunnell, S. Dwight, and Johnson, Donald R. 1974. "Physical factors affecting pika density and dispersal." *Journal of Mammalogy* 55:866–869.

Cowan, Ian McT. 1955. "The distribution of the pikas (*Ochotona*) in British Columbia and Alberta." *Murrelet* 35:20–24.

Dice, Lee R. 1927. "The Colorado pika in captivity." *Journal of Mammalogy* 8:228–231.

Douglas, William O. 1962. "Journey to Outer Mongolia." *National Geographic* 121:289–345.

Ellerman, Sir John R., and Morrison-Scott, T.C.S. 1951. *Checklist of Palaearctic and Indian Mammals, 1758 to 1946.* London. British Museum (Natural History).

Guthrie, Russell D. 1973. "Mummified pika (*Ochotona*) carcass and dung pellets from Pleistocene deposits in interior Alaska." *Journal of Mammalogy* 54:970–971.

Haga, Ryoichi. 1960. "Observations on the ecology of the Japanese pika." *Journal of Mammalogy* 41:200–212.

Hall, E. Raymond, and Kelson, Keith R. 1959. *The Mammals of North America.* 2 vols. New York: Ronald Press.

Harvey, Elmer B., and Rosenberg, Lauren E. 1960. "An apocrine gland complex of the pika." *Journal of Mammalogy* 41:213–219.

Howell, Arthur H. 1924. "Revision of the American pikas (genus *Ochotona*)." *North American Fauna* 47:1–57.

Johnson, Donald R. 1967. "Diet and reproduction of Colorado pikas." *Journal of Mammalogy* 48:311–315.

Kawamichi, Takeo. 1976. "Hay territory and dominance rank of pikas." *Journal of Mammalogy* 57:133–148.

Kilham, Lawrence. 1958. "Territorial behavior in pikas." *Journal of Mammalogy* 39:307.

Kirkpatrick, Jay F., and Satterfield, Virginia. 1973. "Histology and morphology of the female reproductive tract of *Ochotona princeps*." *Journal of Mammalogy* 54:855–861.

Loukashkin, Anatole S. 1940. "On the pikas of north Manchuria." *Journal of Mammalogy* 21:402–405.

Lutton, Lewis M. 1975. "Notes on territorial behavior and response to predators of the pika, *Ochotona princeps*." *Journal of Mammalogy* 56:231–234.

MacArthur, R. A., and Wang, L. C. H. 1973. "Physiology of thermoregulation in the pika, *Ochotona princeps*." *Canadian Journal of Zoology* 51: 11–16.

Markham, O. Doyle, and Whicker, F. W. 1972. "Burrowing in the pika (*Ochotona princeps*)." *Journal of Mammalogy* 53:387–389.

———. 1973. "Notes on the behavior of the pika (*Ochotona princeps*) in captivity." *American Midland Naturalist* 89:192–199.

Millar, John S. 1972. "Timing of breeding of pikas in southwestern Alberta." *Canadian Journal of Zoology* 50:665–669.

―――. 1974. "Success of reproduction in pikas, *Ochotona princeps* (Richardson)." *Journal of Mammalogy* 55:527–542.

Millar, John S., and Zwickel, Fred C. 1972. "Determination of age, age structure, and mortality of the pika, *Ochotona princeps* (Richardson)." *Canadian Journal of Zoology* 50:229–232.

―――. 1972. "Characteristics and ecological significance of hay piles of pikas." *Mammalia* 36:58–68.

Ognev, Sergei I. 1940. *Mammals of the U.S.S.R. and Adjacent Countries.* Translated from Russian. Published for the National Science Foundation, Washington. Jerusalem: Israel Program for Scientific Translations.

Orr, Robert T. 1949. *Mammals of Lake Tahoe.* San Francisco: California Academy of Science.

―――. 1972. "Pikas." *Pacific Discovery* 25 (6):9–11.

Rausch, Robert. 1960. "Notes on the collared pika, *Ochotona collaris* (Nelson), in Alaska." *Murrelet* 42:22–24.

Severaid, J. Harold. 1950. "The gestation period of the pika (*Ochotona princeps*)." *Journal of Mammalogy* 31:356–357.

Index